What people a

A Guide

A serious and erudite examination of the important roles of performing last rites, passing over and preliminary funereal duties. As the author points out, this is not a popular role within Paganism and spirituality generally - it is not for everyone. This book tackles the subject with sensitivity from the point of view of the needs of the dying, rather than the bereaved, and is full of practical advice and help for those wishing to work in this area. **Luke Eastwood**, author of *The Druid's Primer* and *The Journey*

It is a challenging endeavor to present a practical guide to working with a variety of spirits, but Christopher Allaun has proven up for the task in *A Guide of Spirits: A Psychopomp's Manual for Transitioning the Dead to the Afterlife*. He walks the reader through rituals and other techniques for use with a range of spirits, from humans to angels, with finesse. Christopher shares his vast knowledge of different perspectives on spirits and his personal experiences with great ease, which is sure to be a great benefit to the readers. A great overview that is suitable for those new to spirits as well as seasoned practitioners. **Cyndi Brannen**, author of *Keeping Her Keys: An Introduction to Hekate's Modern Witchcraft* and *Entering Hekate's Garden*

In *A Guide of Spirits*, Chris Allaun has created a valuable resource for those interested in psychopomp work who don't have ready access to an in-person mentor. Illustrating his points with anecdotes from his own extensive experience, Allaun provides guidance for every step of the process, from contacting spirit allies to working with the spirit of the deceased to cleansing afterward. Allaun also shares warnings and tips for avoiding trouble and dealing with any problems that may arise, giving the reader a realistic view of this type of spirit work. Altogether, *A Guide of Spirits* is a comprehensive reference for anyone beginning to walk the path of the psychopomp.

Laura Perry, editor of *Deathwalking: Helping Them Cross the Bridge* and author of *Ariadne's Thread: Awakening the Wonders of the Ancient Minoans in Our Modern Lives*

More people are being called to normalize the process of dying and to work with spirits as they move from this life to the next. This call has been growing louder in the last few years. Christopher Allaun's *A Guide of Spirits: A Psychopomp's Manual for Transitioning the Dead to the Afterlife* is his response to this need for knowledge and instruction. His approach and methods in the book are clearly guided by his spirits, his spiritual company, as well as his own experience in this work. The methods and insights presented are specific, well organized, and manage to leave open the way for adjustment to suit the reader's beliefs and background. He speaks from his experience as an example and encourages the reader to find their way forward into the work. Whether you are an old hand or a newcomer you will find insights in *A Guide of Spirits* to improve your practice.

Ivo Dominguez Jr, author of *Keys to Perception: A Practical Guide to Psychic Development*

A fascinating and in depth look at the active side of psychopomp work, this book will guide you through understanding what this work entails and the basics of doing it. From supporting the dying to dealing with haunted places, with an emphasis on healing, Chris Allaun's *A Guide of Spirits* is perfect for beginners or more experienced practitioner.

Morgan Daimler, author of *Fairies: A Guide to the Celtic Fair Folk*

Rich with perspective, balance, and valuable insight, Allaun has broken the mold many books on spirit and ecstatic mediumship fall into and delivers what others have not. *A Guide of Spirits* will be on my recommendation list for years to come.

Devon Hunter, author of *Modern Witch: Spells, Recipes & Workings*

A Guide of Spirits is an in-depth yet accessible exploration of a critical subject that few books go into great detail about; the Psychopomp. In a society where the subject of death is often eschewed and any talk concerning the realms of spirits is given the side-eye, it's far too easy to lose touch with the meaning of life itself and our connection to the Universe. Christopher opens up the door to these mysteries, illuminating them without fluff or being sensational. He provides the reader with a practical guide for how to safely and responsibly interact with spirits and be a means of healing and direction for them in your practice. Definitely a worthwhile read for the magical practitioner seeking to gain greater understanding of what happens after this life and other realms of existence.

Laura Tempest Zakroff, author of *Weave the Liminal*

Throughout history, the role of a psychopomp has been to guide the soul of the deceased through the Afterlife. In our modern world this role is seen as more than that: it is one of also providing spiritual healing and even guidance for the departed. In *A Guide of Spirits: A Psychopomp's Manual for Transitioning the Dead to the Afterlife*, Chris Allaun not only sets out the foundations for anyone wishing to step into this much needed role, but also provides practical insights and exercises into working with ancestors and spirits in general. Incorporating a wonderful blend of mystical as well as magical techniques, you too can become a psychopomp, a guide and healer of souls.

Frances Billinghurst, author of *Dancing the Sacred Wheel: A Journey through the Southern Sabbats and Encountering the Dark Goddess*

A Guide of Spirits

A Psychopomp's Manual for
Transitioning the Dead to the Afterlife

A Guide of Spirits

A Psychopomp's Manual for
Transitioning the Dead to the Afterlife

Chris Allaun

**MOON
BOOKS**

Winchester, UK
Washington, USA

JOHN HUNT PUBLISHING

First published by Moon Books, 2021
Moon Books is an imprint of John Hunt Publishing Ltd., No. 3 East Street, Alresford
Hampshire SO24 9EE, UK
office@jhpbooks.net
www.johnhuntpublishing.com
www.moon-books.net

For distributor details and how to order please visit the 'Ordering' section on our website.

Text copyright: Chris Allaun 2020

ISBN: 978 1 78904 660 1
978 1 78904 661 8 (ebook)
Library of Congress Control Number: 2020942260

A CIP catalogue record for this book is available from the British Library.

Design: Stuart Davies

UK: Printed and bound by CPI Group (UK) Ltd, Croydon, CR0 4YY
Printed in North America by CPI GPS partners

We operate a distinctive and ethical publishing philosophy in
all areas of our business, from our global network of authors to
production and worldwide distribution.

Contents

Acknowledgments   x

Introduction   1

Chapter 1: The Psychopomp   5

Chapter 2: Psychopomp Teachers   20

Chapter 3: The Afterlife   42

Chapter 4: Spirit Communication   62

Chapter 5: Helping the Dying to Transition   84

Chapter 6: Working with the Spirits   109

Chapter 7: Earthbound   131

Chapter 8: Guiding the Spirit   146

Chapter 9: Haunted Houses and Psychic Self-Defense   174

Conclusion   203

Acknowledgements

I would like to take this opportunity to say thank you to a few people.

First and foremost I would like to say thank you to everyone at Moon Books for allowing me to share my magick with all of you.

I would like to thank my physical teachers Matthew Ellenwood, Billie Topa Tate, and many others who have taught me magick and healing along the way.

Also, thank you to my teachers in spirit, my gods, my ancestors, and the healing spirits who walk with me upon this sacred path.

A very special thank you to John Hijatt for doing the first edits of this book with me. He is a master at his craft and I cannot thank him enough!

Lastly, I want to thank all of you who have supported my books, my classes, articles, and video blogs over the years. Thank you so much. Always.

Introduction

Working with the spirits of the dead is one of the most rewarding things you can do as a healer. Many people are under the impression that once a person transitions into death and leave their body that they find themselves in a place of bliss and happiness. This may certainly be the case for some, but not for all. There are many reasons that someone may stay behind on the earth plane and not journey to the Land of the Ancestors. To guide the spirits into the afterlife is sacred healing work. It is an act of kindness to help those people cross the veil to be reunited with their beloved ancestors. Psychopomps depicted in art and movies are often painted as dark shadowy figures who take spirits into the foggy realms of the Underworld. This is far from the truth. The psychopomp is a healer who helps the spirits of the dead find balance and healing as they journey to the afterlife where they will find renewal.

It is my hope that this book will take out some of the mystery of guiding the spirits and fill you with a sense of wonder and magick as you do this sacred work. I wrote this book because I wanted to share my experiences and magical techniques with those who feel drawn to working with the spirits of the dead. After I wrote my first book, *Underworld: Shamanism, Myth, and Magick,* I found that there were many people who wanted to help the dead cross over to the Land of the Ancestors but did not necessarily know how. They would explain to me that they had a calling to help the spirits on their journey, but they were not sure how to take the first steps. My other intention in writing this book is to take away the stigma of darkness of the psychopomp. Don't get me wrong. I enjoy the shadowy aspects of magick as much as the next person, but psychopomp work is about helping spirits continue on their spiritual journey and find their happiness.

We begin this book by learning about what a psychopomp is and how we heal the spirits of the dead. Once someone dies and shed their physical form they are often forgotten. It is the psychopomp who is called to perform the sacred duty of guiding the spirits back home to their beloved ancestors. Once we understand the role of the psychopomp we must begin our spiritual journey and learn from our teacher in spirit. Living teachers are wonderful but can only teach us so much. It is the gods, spirit guides, ancestors, and spirit teachers who will teach us the deeper lessons of healing and the realms of the afterlife. The land of the dead, sometimes called the afterlife, is a wonderful place that reunites the spirits with their beloved ancestors. In order for us to successfully learn to be a guide to the spirits we must learn about the land of the dead and how it is a place of healing and rejuvenation.

For many of us it is difficult to communicate with the spirits. It is important to be able to effectively speak with the spirits so that we can help them on their journey home. In this book, you will be given steps to develop your inherent ability to talk to each spirit you come in contact with. In the following chapter we will learn to aid the dying as they transition into death. As energy healers we have the ability to support the dying in their final moments of life and be with them as they shed their physical body in order to take the journey into the spiritual realms. We will also learn to deepen our psychic skills and learn how to see and hear the spirits in a clear tangible way. I will give you several magical techniques that will strengthen your psychic abilities so that you will be able to talk with the spirits clearly and effectively.

In the last part of this book, we will learn about the many different reasons why the dead do not cross over. It is not our responsibility to judge the spirit of the dead, but it is our duty to help them the best way we can. I have written the stories of several people who have died and either could not or would not cross over to the afterlife. These are real stories taken from my own personal experience of working with the dead. I will also give you a psychopomp ceremony and step by step directions on how to guide the spirit into the afterlife so they may find the healing they need. Lastly, there will be instances where you will be called out to assist in clearing a home that is haunted by restless spirits. Most of the time it is easy to clear spirits who are causing havoc in someone's home. There will be times, however, where a difficult spirit will refuse to journey across the veil. I will give you techniques and ceremonies on how to help difficult spirits find their way back to the Land of the Ancestors.

This book is a compilation of my experience of guiding the spirits of the dead back home to be with their ancestors and find healing and renewal. I have been doing this work for over 20 years and I can say this is the most gratifying healing work that I perform. Even if you are not called to work with the dead full time, this book will serve as a manual on how to guide the dead should the need arise in your spiritual practice. May you walk with the spirits with grace and dignity.

Chapter 1

The Psychopomp

"Let thoughts of love, not grief, follow that soul upon its journey, as sea-gulls follow a ship. Let us bid him God-speed and good cheer, and look forward to the reunion." -Dion Fortune, *Through the Gates of Death*

Psychopomps as Healers

I believe that everyone has the potential to be a healer. We are born into this physical existence to help each other progress on our spiritual paths. Not all healers are the same. The type of healing you do is as individual as you are. Many people have the idea that a healer is either an energy worker that sees many clients a day in a private practice or a doctor who operates on us when our bodies are cut or damaged. These things are certainly aspects of healing, but there is much more to helping someone find wellbeing than this. As an example, there are healers who are massage therapists, reiki masters, acupuncturists, nurses, psychologists, counselors, and spiritual leaders. We are also healers when we are good friends, parents, teachers, and partners. What makes someone a healer is not what title they hold, but having compassion for someone else in their time of need. I define a healer as someone who does the best they can to help others while having compassion and connecting to the Universe. We are more than our physical bodies. We are spiritual, energetic, and emotional beings who walk upon our paths the best we can. There are many healers now who are using the term *holistic healing*. What this means is that, not only are we treating the physical bodies for illness, we are also treating the energy, mental, emotional, and spiritual bodies as well.

Healing is needed many times in our life. We need healers when we are born. The midwife or doctor help our mothers in the birth process. They also help us as infants to make sure we are as healthy as possible as we begin our new lives. As children, we need healing when we fall and hurt ourselves. This healing often comes from the love of parents and the compassion of teachers. As we grow up, we receive healing in many different ways. Sometimes we receive healing from the compassion of a friend, or a life lesson well learned. As we grow older, we need the aid of healers when we break a bone, need surgery, or need emotional and energy healing when life becomes overwhelming. We often need the aid of spiritual healers when we question the Universe and the gods. At the end of our lives, the healing energies of the psychopomp will help us transition into the spirit world and find our way into the Land of the Ancestors. In the pagan tradition that I follow, it is believed that upon death the ancestors will aid you in your transition into the afterlife. The ancestors will fill you with the energies of love and compassion and guide you to a place of rest and renewal where your line of ancestors await your arrival. There are many times that the deceased may need healing as they transition into death and go forward upon the path leading to the afterlife. When the physical body is shed, the spirit retains the normal consciousness of the person just as when they were alive. They still have the hopes, dreams, fears, and biases they had in life. What this means, however, is they will also have the emotional and psychological issues that occurred in their life at the time of death. There are many challenges and lessons that we may endure as we walk upon our spiritual path. From some of these challenges, we will learn valuable lessons and continue to heal. Other challenges will be traumatic for various reasons and will cause us pain. At the time of death, a person's spirit will process the energies in the best way it can. That being said, there are times that the spirit of the dead will choose not to transition into the afterlife and remains bound to the physical plane for a variety of reasons. It is important that the spirit receive healing when this occurs and is guided by a psychopomp to the afterlife.

A psychopomp is a special type of healer. Not only do they escort the spirit of the dead to the realm of the ancestors, they also send the spirit healing energy to aid in letting go of earthly attachments that may keep them bound to the physical world. The word itself comes from the Greek language which roughly translates to "conductor" or "guide" of the soul. To me, psychopomp work is about helping the spirits of the dead make the journey to the Land of the Ancestors in a way that shows them compassion. Another aspect of psychopomp work is Death Midwifery. This is very sacred work and for many people who you help transition into death, this may be the last act of healing they experience from a living human being. Some healers call themselves *death midwives* or *death doulas* when they are helping someone transition and *psychopomp* when they are aiding in the journey to the spirit world. When someone is transitioning into death, it is important to remember that they are experiencing the death process alone. It is true that you may be by their side during the time of death, but they are having an experience that is unique to them. Our job at this time is to give energy only when needed and guided by our spirit guides and ancestors. It is also important to be present for them whereby the act of holding sacred space can sometimes help in the transition process. In her book *The Art of Death Midwifery: An Introduction and Beginner's Guide,* Joellyn St. Pierre says:

> "The art of death midwifery is a profound and intuitive way of communing with the dying, of lending support and guidance to those making this greatest of transitions. Committing to deep spiritual work, the death midwife becomes a strong, clear conduit who directs the flow of divine love to the dying."

The performance of psychopomp work is an act of compassion to which few are drawn because many people fear and avoid death, and have not come to terms with dying. Assisting in the death process and helping someone cross over can be overwhelming. For numerous people who are in hospitals experiencing the death process, it can feel lonely and isolating. Some families will gather around the dying and be present with them. Others, however, will not. I have often heard someone say, "I want to remember them the way they were". I do not place judgement on where someone is when it comes to assisting the dying as that is for them to decide. Also, doctors and nurses have extremely limited time when it comes to visiting and checking up on the dying. I had a friend who was a hospice doctor. She was instructed by her supervisors to spend no more than a few minutes with each person every day. Some of her patients wanted to talk with her a moment longer, but she was not allowed. She got fired one day for spending too much time with her patients. These patients wanted just a little moment or two longer than she was told to give. They said she was not using her time wisely. For those who are dying, every moment is precious and sometimes human connection is all they need. For those of us as psychopomps and healers, we have the ability to be present with the dying. Our job is more than energy healing and spirit walking. It is having compassion for those who need us. It is also the act of being present and witnessing someone's transition into the next part of their journey.

As a witch and Spirit Walker, I have always been drawn to the dead. They have been around me my whole life and I can always feel their presence. It is important to my spiritual practice to perform psychopomp work when needed. For me, it is a calling. However, I feel that anyone can do this type of work with the right guidelines and practice. You do not have to be a spiritual leader or have several certifications in energy healing, shamanism, or degrees in witchcraft. Anyone can be taught to do this sacred work. The only requirement is to practice the energy techniques I will give you in this book as well as have compassion for the dying and the spirits of the dead. Above all else, however, you will need to work with your ancestors, spirit guides, and gods. I am only a teacher and a guide. The spirits who assist you in this work will be the ones who give you the most teaching. We will talk about that more later in this book.

Psychopomp work is a very sacred and healing practice. There will be times when you will need to use energy healing to help the spirit leave the body in a whole and loving way. There will be times when you will need to heal certain aspects of the astral and energy bodies in order for the person to let go of earthly attachments so they can go on their journey while in a place of balance. There will also be many times when you will be asked to escort the dead to the realm of the ancestors so that they can be home with their families in spirit. However, there will be many times with this sacred work that you will only need to be present. Perhaps you will only be needed to hear someone's story or to simply fill the room with compassion and love. Each person's needs are different. The role of the psychopomp is to be a conduit of healing and compassion during this sacred time.

The Call of the Dead

When I was little, I could feel the spirits of the dead around me. I never knew a time when they were not near. I could not see them as I would see a living person, but I knew they were there by feeling their presence and connecting to their emotions. I could understand their wants and desires as well as their hopes and fears. I tried to dismiss these feelings as my imagination. There were times when I could feel a great need in the spirits. The dark would hold their emotional pain. It was not the darkness of night that alarmed me, it was that the dead were near, and I was too young to understand what they wanted. As I grew up, I became interested in magick, witchcraft, and Spirit Walking. I studied as much magick as I could. During my studies, the dead were always near. It seemed to me that they were watching my progress. Maybe. Maybe not. That is just what it felt like at the time. My teachers said I had an affinity to the Underworld and the ancestors. Or was it that the dead had an affinity towards me? The dead began to call to me. They began to appear to me, asking me for help. I did not really understand how to help them heal and cross over to the spirit world. During the 90's and early 2000's I did not find many people who knew much about guiding the spirits of the dead, so I had to rely on my teachers in spirit. There were also few books that taught this type of work. With the instructions of the spirits, and then later my shamanic teachers, I was able to answer the call of the dead.

Some people will be drawn to this type of spiritual healing. Not for the delight of the macabre, but because they are healers and the spirits of the dead need healing as well. Many healers have a need to help and guide others. We have a need to do healing work because either we understand what it is like to be in need or we are able to feel the emotions of those who desperately need our help. Being a healer is a calling. I have come to understand that all healers have a higher vibration in our auras and energy bodies that can be seen in the spirit world. It is our glow of compassion and healing that draws us ever closer to the spirits of the dead who need our help. It is our path we must journey on and to follow this path leads to balance for ourselves and the world around us.

Not everyone will feel the call to be a psychopomp, but this work is important for everyone. Death is a part of life and life is a part of death. In paganism and witchcraft, we often speak about the cycle of birth, life, death, and rebirth. The cycle of life and death never ends. It is a constant throughout the Universe. Each of us has known someone who has died. We cannot escape death. The more we understand the process and the purpose of death, the more understanding we will have of the Universe as well as ourselves. Death is a rite of passage. Just as we celebrate birth, adulthood, weddings, and retiring, so should we celebrate and honor the death of someone. Death is the great transition into the afterlife and to the next life after that. We should not hide from it or put it out of our site. We should honor death and help people through it the best we can.

The energy healing techniques of the psychopomp can create a beautiful experience for both the dying and for yourself. This is a sacred act that will help a person who is transitioning into death heal and find their way to the realm of the ancestors. When we are born into this world we are not alone. We have the magick of our mother and many other people who help in the birthing process. Just as we assist the newborn in birth, it is equally important to help the dying person find their way into the afterlife to begin the next part of their sacred journey.

The Transition of Death

There are different ideas of what happens during the transition into death. From those people who have clinically died and are resuscitated, there have been reports of seeing a light at the end of the tunnel as well as seeing one's ancestors and gods. Scientists have explained this phenomenon with a few different theories. One theory says that it is simply a lack of blood to the brain. Another theory states that there are many endorphins that are released from the brain at the point of death. According to the article "Are near-death experiences hallucinations? Experts explain the science behind this puzzling phenomenon", authors Neil Dagnall and Ken Drinkwater say, "But, the most widespread explanation for near death experiences is the *dying brain hypothesis*. This theory proposes that near death experiences are hallucinations caused by activity in the brain as the brain cells begin to die."

I have come to believe, that even if these scientific things are occurring in the brain at the time of death, that the spiritual experiences are just as valid and real. How is it that we are able to have a religious experience? James Giordano is a neuropathologist who has done extensive research in brain function during religious mystical experiences. Giordano says that mystical experiences are first activated in the brainstem, or the reptilian brain, with a sense of heightened arousal. Once this occurs, the midbrain, the limbic system, then releases opioid peptides allowing the brain to experience a great increase in pleasure. The brain then experiences the spiritual occurrence when the amygdala in the limbic system is activated to bring a sense of intensity to the experience while the hippocampus fires to give us a feeling of spirituality. It is true that in order for us to experience the ancestors and the spirits, certain aspects of the physical brain must fire in order for us to feel and observe the experience. But it does not mean that the feeling of spirit is only in our heads. In order for us to really feel and observe the spiritual experience, we need the complex functions of the brain to act as a conduit of spiritual energy. Just as we need our nerves to feel heat, cold, pain, and pleasure, we need our physical brains to experience spiritual energy. So, in conclusion, just as our brains are needed to experience religious occurrences such as magick, the ancestors, and the gods, so too are our brains needed to experience the spiritual aspect of the death process. Both are just as valid as the other.

When someone is close to death, many times they will begin seeing their ancestors and those whom they loved who have passed on. They may even see beloved pets from their life. This happens because their life force is waning, and they are becoming closer to the world of spirit. This also happens sometimes because the closer a person gets to death, the more their bodies begin to break down. The person may become cold, lethargic, have low energy, and become less focused. Not everyone experiences the death process in the same way, so everyone will have a different experience. One of the reasons a dying person begins to see their ancestors is because it helps them transition in a gentler way. When someone sees their loved ones who have died, it helps them understand that there is life after death and they will soon join them.

When the spirit leaves the body upon death it is said that they will be greeted by the ancestors, beloved friends, pets, gods, and guardian spirits they may have had during life. There are several purposes for this: many people are afraid to die or are anxious about death and wonder if there is life after death at all; others wonder if their spiritual beliefs were wrong and that at death they will cease to exist. The ancestors will help with that anxiety.

Another reason for them to appear is to help guide them to the afterlife. How I have experienced this in my psychopomp work, is that a portal is opened at the time of death and the ancestors and spirits appear. They then take the spirit of the deceased through the energy portal back to the realm of the ancestors. Then the portal closes. I have not seen the light and the tunnel that is said in near death experiences. However, I have come to believe that, as with all spiritual things, everyone has a unique experience. The stories that are written in myth and lore are just some of the scenarios that may happen upon death.

The transition into death is a beautiful experience, but not everyone who is at the point of death may face energies the same way. Some may have great fear or doubts about going through the portal. They may even have unfinished business or other reasons why they do not want to go through the portal into the afterlife. In our lives we have free will. We make our own choices with each crossroad that we come to upon our journey. Death is no different. The spirits cannot force us to do anything we do not want to do. If we choose to stay earthbound, then we will stay earthbound either until we are ready to journey into the afterlife or unless a psychopomp helps guide us. Perception is another factor. If someone dies suddenly such as in a traffic accident, a drive by shooting, or of a sudden heart attack, they may not realize they are dead. They may also be angry about their death and are unwilling to accept it as reality. Because of this, they may not even see the ancestors and the portal to the afterlife. This may sound strange, but how many times have you walked by a picture, vase, or statue somewhere and said, "Has this always been there?" Your consciousness will only see what it is ready to see. The person who has died may choose on some level not to see the path to the afterlife. This is also one of the many reasons psychopomp work is needed.

The Afterlife

In paganism, the afterlife is seen as the realm of the ancestors. It is seen as a beautiful place where the spirit of the deceased is reunited with their beloved ancestors, dear friends, and pets they once had in life. It is here that your ancestors welcome you into the energetic bloodline of your family heritage. This is also the place where you will review your life and learn from the lessons you were given on the physical plane. Above all, the realm of the ancestors is a place to heal from the wounds of life and enjoy the presence and love of family and friends. Many witches and pagans believe in reincarnation. We believe that the spirit will be reborn again on the physical plane in order to continue the spiritual lessons needed to become a fully enlightened being. We believe that one human lifetime is not enough time to learn the many lessons that the Universe has for us. So, we must be reborn time and time again until we have evolved into such a state of enlightenment. Once our consciousness has reached the enlightened state, we can choose to remain with the beloved ancestors as teacher and guide, or we may ascend to the celestial realm in order to become teacher and guide in spirit for the world. Being reincarnated means that our time in the realm of the ancestors is limited. We will only be there long enough to heal, renew our spirit, and to understand the lessons we were taught on Earth.

Not all pagans and witches believe in this aspect of the afterlife. There are many different spiritual paths in paganism, and each has their own view on what happens upon death. In the Wiccan tradition they call the afterlife the Summerland because it is thought to be a place of forever summer. No winter or fall, only perpetual bliss of warmth and light. This is a place of great joy and love. In the Heathen community there are a couple of places one may go to upon death. There is also the idea of the world of Helheim. This is the world of the dead in the Underworld located in the roots of the great tree Yggdrasil. Helheim is governed by the great goddess Hela. The way she appears to me, her face is half that of a beautiful maiden and half of a decaying skull. In his book *The Pathwalker's Guide To the Nine Worlds,* Raven Kaldera explains how the goddess of death, Hela, lovingly takes care of the dead in her great hall:

"There is something strongly maternal about Hela's care for her charges, even though she is no mother goddess. Her love is impersonable, but constant, and visitors are also considered under her care and will not go hungry unless they offend her."

Heathens believe that their fallen warriors are chosen by either the God Odin or the Goddess Freya to live with them in their mighty Halls in Asgard, the Nordic Upperworld. Each day the warriors enjoy fighting each other in battle while each night is feasting and drinking.

In Greek mythology there is the Underworld land of Hades. Hades is named after the Greek god of the Underworld who shares the same name. This place is ruled both by Hades and his beloved Queen, Persephone. The afterlife of the Greeks was a place that was mostly dark and covered in shadow. However, for some special people, such as heroes, poets, healers, and leaders, there was Elysium. This was a place of beauty, warmth, and bliss that is more akin to the Wiccan Summerland. In some Traditional Witchcraft circles there is the belief that once the witch has died, they are transported to the Rose Castle. This is a dilapidated castle that is vacant and is lost to shadow. But, to those who call out to the Witch Goddess and know the nature of death and the afterlife, the wasteland turns into a beautiful bright castle that is surrounded by roses. It is here that the Witch Goddess takes the witch to the afterlife. The Egyptians have the Underworld land of the Duat. The Duat is a mirror reflection of the physical plane but is a place that tests the newly deceased to make sure that their hearts are pure before being admitted to a place of eternal joy. Then there are the Buddhist spirit worlds that contain many places of gods, hungry ghosts, and frightening creatures who are a manifestation of the spirit's hopes and fears.

I have journeyed many times to the shamanic Underworld. In my spirit travels, I have discovered that the realm of the ancestors is wonderous, vast, and diverse. This is because the Underworld is a place that is made up of energy. When we take our last breath, we will shed our physical body and be taken to the realm of the ancestors. We will be united with our beloved dead and be welcomed home to our families. But what does the world of the dead look like? Is it the dark shadowing place that is described in Greek mythology or is it a place that is filled with perpetual fog? I have found that the Underworld Land of the Ancestors is exactly what you think it is going to be. The ancestral lands will take its shape according to your desires, culture, and upbringing. For many witches and pagans, the Land of the Ancestors is a beautiful place of warmth, joy, and rejuvenation.

Your mind is very powerful and has the ability to shape your reality. More accurately, your mind has the power to shape your perceived reality. Tibetan Buddhists understand this concept quite well. When a Buddhist is close to death, they are instructed to visualize their spirit leaving the body through the crown chakra. By doing this, they avoid any unwanted karma and enter the energy world of the afterlife with a clear spirit. The Tibetan Book of the Dead is read to the newly deceased so that the spirit can face their fears, avoid demonic creatures, and focus on *liberation*, the release from the karmic wheel of life, death, and rebirth. They understand that the gods and monsters they encounter upon the death journey are simply manifestations of their own consciousness. In Spirit Walking, we often create our own environment that we see during our journeys. This is why many students who are beginning to learn journeying ask if they are making up their journeys. What I teach my students is that the three shamanic worlds are *both* real and a product of your imagination. You may be asking yourself, how is this so?

It is said that the witch and Spirit Walker creates their own world. We manifest our desires by many different means. Sometimes we cast spells or hold rituals. Other times, we drum and sing sacred songs to bring in healing energies. There are also times when we sit in meditation and call upon universal energies to empower our desires. In every one of these instances, you are sending energy to an outcome that you have visualized. In magick and healing, you cannot obtain your desired outcome without visualizing. When we visualize, we are creating form on the astral plane. This is basically what we call a thought form. A thought form can only maintain its form on the astral plane a short time unless it is empowered with energy. Once the thought form has sufficient energy, then the Universe will manifest the desire for you. I like to think of it like I am programming the Universe with my intended desire just as you would program a computer to give you your intended desire.

When we die, we shed our physical bodies and our spiritual bodies are taken to the energetic world of the ancestors in the

Underworld. At death, we hold our individual consciousness, but we are essentially a form of spiritual energy. Being in the spirit world we are directly in contact with the astral and spiritual energies of the Universe. Our thoughts, especially our subconscious thoughts that we have been collecting our whole lives, impact the energetic environment around us and shape our world. So, however we perceive the afterlife, this is how it will appear. It is shaped by our thoughts even if we are not aware of it. This is why when someone dies, they see the realm of the ancestors as they believe it will be. This is why to the ancient Greeks, the afterlife looks like Hades, to the Egyptians the afterlife looks like the lush landscape of the Nile river, and to Heathens the afterlife looks like a great hall.

Attachment to Physical Life

During the transition of death, the dying should try to let go of all earthly attachments and focus on Spirit. The reason for this is because all thoughts have magical power. Each thought that we have, both positive and negative, has the ability to influence our physical reality. This is more than "think good thoughts and good things will happen to you". What this means is that we shape our world with our beliefs, hopes, fears, and desires. Often times, what we fear we manifest in our reality in order to learn from this fear. We also manifest what we greatly desire. Have you ever wanted something so much that you did whatever it took to obtain the object of your desire? Essentially, this is magick. Our thoughts are powerful and when we attach deeply strong emotions to those thoughts then we are adding a great deal of power to them.

At death, if we hold on to great attachment of "worldly" things, the thoughts and emotions that we have will energetically bind us to the physical plane. By doing our best to release our earthly attachments, there will be no energetic chords that will keep us from transitioning to the afterlife. When I was first learning this concept, I was a bit confused because I thought that non-attachment meant that you did not have love for the people who were important to you during your life. I learned that this is far from the truth. When someone is transitioning into death, you still love your loved ones; but you are trusting that they will be taken care of by the Universe and the people you leave behind. One of the roles of the psychopomp is to help the spirit heal from attachments that keep them from moving to the realm of the ancestors.

Psychopomp work is a wonderful and sacred healing modality. By doing this work, you are participating in profound spiritual events. It is a great honor and privilege to be able to guide someone from the last event of their physical life to their next journey into the spirit world. It is also a great honor simply to be present and bear witness to the beautiful experience that we call death. With this work, the dying can go forward into their transition with the understanding that you will be with them all the way. They will be comforted by the fact that they are not alone. You will be able gently guide them back home to the Land of the Ancestors.

Chapter 2

Psychopomp Teachers

We will have many teachers as we walk the winding road of our spiritual path. There will be times that we learn from books and other magical practitioners and then there will be times we learn from the spirits themselves. We learn many valuable things from other magical people. I love meeting new people who practice their craft in a different way than I do. I love trading ideas and techniques and having discussions of magical and spiritual philosophy. There is a vast spiritual and magical community out there with many talented and likeminded people. When I teach classes and private students, I learn a great deal from them. Even beginners can show us a new approach to something or see a technique in a whole new way. Many practitioners will reach a point in their development where they will need formal study with seasoned teachers. Teachers are a vital part of magical practice. They help us learn discipline and hold us accountable to the path that we chose to follow. Human teachers are a wonderful place to start. Yes, to start. A good teacher will help you acquire a good magical foundation but will not do the work for you. They will show you were the path is, but you have to walk it to the best of your ability.

As amazing as human teachers are, the best teachers I have found are the spirits. The spirits have a deeper connection to the otherworld and have experiences that we humans can never have. Even with years of experience with spirit work, spirits have an understanding of the energies and the secrets of the Universe that we can never have without their help. As a witch and Spirit Walker you will have many spirit teachers. There are spirits who guide us in the Upperworld, the Otherworld, and the Underworld. I recommend that anyone who journeys in the three shamanic worlds find a spirit teacher for each world. For psychopomp work, you will not only need an ancestral teacher, but you will need a Psychopomp Teacher who is spirit as well.

The Psychopomp Teacher will give you the needed training and mentoring that a physical teacher can never give you. This book will help you start on the path of the psychopomp and give you many useful magical techniques and ideas but a Psychopomp Teacher will show you the deeper magical mysteries of this work that I could never could. One of the benefits of having a teacher or mentor is that they can monitor your progress and give you feedback. Your Psychopomp Teacher will create a teaching plan that is designed around you. They will teach you techniques according to your magical and spiritual skill level. I have found that our spirit teachers are very patient with us because they understand our human failings. They will not rush us to speed through a technique so we can rush into the next one and they will not fault us if we are not ready to go forward. They will meet us at our skill level and prompt us to go forward when we are ready.

The Psychopomp Teacher is a part of the energy worlds and they will have the ability to see energies that we may not be able to see. Also, time and space flows differently in the spirit worlds so they will be able to see things in the past, present, and future which allows them to have a better perspective on things. There have been times I wanted to help a spirit of the dead cross over and my Psychopomp Teacher had the foresight to know that that was not the right time because the spirit had more lessons to learn on the physical plane. These are wonderful benefits that will really help our psychopomp healing sessions. Your Psychopomp Teacher spirit is vital for your continuing growth and evolution upon the path of healing the spirits of the dead.

The Psychopomp Teacher can be a spirit of the dead, a god or goddess, an animal spirit, an angel, or ascended ancestor. Each of us has our own spiritual path that we should design to fit our individual beliefs and spiritual needs. The Psychopomp Teacher that we work with should resonate with the spiritual path that we follow. It does not matter what kind of spirit your teacher is. The important thing is that they are teaching you the spiritual skills that you will need in order to perform your psychopomp work. Your teacher will be able to help you heal the transitioning spirit and assist you in escorting the dead to the afterlife, as well as navigating the Land of the Ancestors. Just as with other spirits we work with, it is more likely that the spirit will choose us rather than us choosing them.

When looking for your Psychopomp Teacher it may be helpful to think about what spirits resonate with you. As an example, what spiritual path are you currently following? For myself, I follow Greco-Roman, Traditional Witchcraft, Norse, and Native American. Another question is, what spirits do you resonate with from your path? I have always had a connection to Hekate and Azrael. I do not have them on my god altar in my home. It never felt quite right for that, but I do have them on my altar of death. That feels very right for me. My advice on finding your Psychopomp Teacher is to go on a journey with the spirits. This is similar to journeying to find your Spirit Animal or your helper spirits in the otherworlds. Another thing to keep in mind is do not be surprised if your Psychopomp Teacher turns out to be a spirit from a completely different path than the one you are following. The Universe, or more correctly the Multiverse, is vast and full of possibilities. Anything can and will happen.

Your Psychopomp Teacher can certainly be gods, angels, or other advanced beings, but they may actually be any type of spirit that is able to guide you in your work. Some of the best magical training I have received came from spirits that I had never heard of. It may sound glamorous to say that our teacher is no other than the Angel of Death, but you can find many powerful teachers who are not gods or angels. In the traditional witchcraft path that I follow, we work quite heavily with the witch ancestors, sometimes called the "Hidden Company". These are spirits of witches who lend their magick to our workings when called upon and can guard your rites from outside forces. There are many teachers among the witch ancestors who can help us with psychopomp work. Not all psychopomps were witches in life. There are many teachers in spirit who were Spirit Walkers, healers, and necromantic magicians who can also help us on our path. The important thing to remember when you are deciding what spirit to work with as a teacher is their ability to teach and guide you in your spiritual work.

In this chapter, I am presenting just some of the more common deities who act as psychopomps for the dead. I am giving just a sample of a few deities and spirits from different cultures. The reason I give a small sample of different cultures, is that many readers have their own unique paths and follow a different culture than I do. By no means is this a complete list of the spiritual beings who have escorted the dead to the afterlife. I will encourage you to work with one or more of these spirits to help you with your psychopomp skills. If you find that these spirits do not resonate with your path, please feel free to research and honor deities who are more congruent to your spiritual path and cosmology. There are many different pagan paths and many of them have a psychopomp of some kind that leads the dead to the ancestral realms. . One thing to remember is that gods, goddesses, and spirits may have different attributes in different cultures at different times in history. For example, the goddess Diana was worshiped in parts of the Middle East, Greece, Rome, and many other places. Each of these cultures worshiped her in their own way. No one culture is more correct than another. They may have just seen an aspect of her energies differently than neighboring people.

Hekate

One of the most famous psychopomps in the pagan world is the goddess Hekate. We often think of Hekate as the dark crone goddess of the Underworld who leads the dead into the darkness of Hades. Yet, Hekate is so much more than this. She is the goddess of the crossroads, witchcraft, necromancy, liminal spaces, gateways, households, initiation into the mysteries, and many other things. She is often associated with Persephone and Demeter. This is one of the reasons that modern witches associate her with the crone. Persephone being the maiden, Demeter the mother, and Hekate the crone. She is also associated with Artemis and Selene. It is not difficult to see that her powers over witchcraft, necromancy, and the Underworld link her to the waning and dark moon so, therefore, she is associated with the crone. However, she was normally perceived as a young vibrant woman, both fierce and beautiful. The idea that Hekate is a crone was only established in the 20th Century. Sorita d'Este, in her wonderful book *Circle For Hekate: Volume 1: History and Mythology* says:

> "It is evident that Hekate manifested in different forms at different times and places throughout history, so it is entirely possible that she is able to reveal herself in new manifestations to devotees today. It can be challenging and sometimes emotional to put aside the conditioning and presumptions passed on to us by our teachers, however doing so can often open up much wider and often more interesting perspectives."

She is depicted as three goddesses in one or sometimes a goddess with three different heads. Sometimes her head is depicted as a woman and other times as the head of an animal such as a cow, horse, snake, or dog. All of these animals are sacred to her. In her hands she holds keys, torches, and a serpent. It is important to understand that she is depicted somewhat differently in art and statues depending on the energies the artist was connecting to and, of course, the regions they were in. The tools which Hekate wields are highly rich in function, symbolism, and magick. The key that she holds has the power to open the gates between the worlds. This allows the witch to travel into the Upperworld, the Midworld, and the Underworld. This is also one of the reasons she is the goddess of the crossroads. Her keys open the gates of Hades itself as well as the doors that hold the mysteries of initiation and the secrets of the Universe. Her torches are symbolic of the light of the moon and the stars. Her mother is named Asteria and is a goddess of the stars, thus linking Hekate with the powers of the celestial realms. Her torches are also the light that leads Persephone to and from Hades linking her to the divine psychopomp. It is interesting to note that oftentimes in mythology, torches are the source of enlightenment because they show light (knowledge and wisdom) in the darkness (ignorance and short sightedness). The serpent holds much power and symbolism as well. To ancient pagans, serpents are symbols of energy and healing. When we view energy with psychic focus it often resembles a serpent sliding upon the ground. Also, it is interesting to note that Asclepius, the god of healing, carries a staff with a serpent coiled around it. The serpent also represents Hekate's chthonic nature in that snakes often live in holes deep in the earth. This once again associates her with the powers of the Underworld. In her book, *Keeping Her Keys: An Introduction to Hekate's Modern Witchcraft*, Cyndi Brannen says:

"From the ancient sources, we know that Hekate was a liminal goddess, standing between the worlds, particularly at the threshold of life and death. She was described in many diverse ways including Mother of All, Savior and World

Soul. She was viewed as the torch bearing guide for those on nightmarish Under World journeys. Not only was she viewed as the guide along the road, but also as the way itself."

In Greek mythology, Hekate was originally a Titan. But when Zeus rebelled against his father, Kronos, Hekate joined him in the great war. Zeus rewarded her loyalty and service with the powers over the three worlds. Another important myth surrounding Hekate is the kidnapping of Persephone by Hades. In the myth, the maiden Persephone was picking flowers by a mountain when it opened up and out sprang Hades, who took her upon his mighty chariot and stole her away to the Underworld. It was only Hekate who heard her cries. Hekate accompanied Persephone's mother, Demeter, when she spoke to the sun god, Helios, and discovered that it was Hades who took her daughter away. She then petitioned Zeus to intervene and it was discovered that Persephone had eaten the pomegranate seeds in Hades and therefore could not leave the subterranean realm. Because Demeter threatened an eternal winter, Hades compromised and allowed Persephone to be with her mother six months out of the year. To this day, it is Hekate who guides Persephone down to the Underworld and back again with her torches.

Another reason that Hekate is viewed as psychopomp is because of her association with the dead. She is a goddess of gates and doorways. Nothing was able to pass through without her permission. These places were thought to be in between the worlds because they were in between inside and outside or between your home and the outside world. Because of this, energetically, doorways were also in-between this world and the spirit world. Spirits of the dead were thought to congregate outside near doorways and gates. Because of this, Hekate had control over the passageways that could allow the dead to go to and from their point of interest. It is interesting to note that

Hekate was also seen as the goddess of the unwanted dead. The Greeks believed that if the dead were not buried with proper funeral rites, they were not allowed through the gates of Hades. These spirits would wait outside the gates until they were allowed inside. Because of Hekate's control over the gates, the unwanted dead were associated with her.

Hermes

Hermes is the son of the mighty Zeus and of Maia, one of the seven Pleiades. He is the messenger of the gods and is the only god able to travel to all three of the worlds. He is a psychopomp who is often associated with Hekate. Both of these deities are gods of gates and boundaries and lead the spirits of the dead into the Underworld of Hades. Hermes is not only a psychopomp, he is also the god of shepherds, thieves, merchants, and good fortune. To many people, he is known as a trickster god. In mythology, on the day he was born he used his great power of speed to steal the cattle of his brother, Apollo. In *The Homeric Hymns*, translated by Diane J. Rayor, The Hymn To Hermes says:

> Maia bore a wily child with a seductive mind-
> A robber, a cattle rustler, guide of dreams
> Who stands watch by night, guardian at the gate
> Who would soon reveal glorious deeds among immortal
> gods
> Born at dawn, at midday played the lyre,
> At dusk he stole the cattle of Apollo the skillful archer

His mighty tools consist of the winged shoes, the winged hat, and the caduceus. The winged shoes and hat, of course, give him the power to speed through the Universe giving messages to gods and mortal people alike. Because of this, he is able to fly down to the Underworld of Hades and speak with Hades.

When Demeter wanted Persephone back, Zeus sent Hermes down to Hades to tell the Underworld god to release her back to her mother. Hermes is often depicted as a kind god, but he delights in trickery. Trickster gods have an important role to play in the Universe. They are not merely gods who delight in hurting people. On the contrary, trickster gods and spirits have the divine purpose of playing tricks on us so that they may teach us a valuable lesson or divine gift. After Hermes stole Apollo's cattle, he gifted him a lyre that played the most beautiful music. Tricksters essentially help us fall on our faces so that we may be humble and pick ourselves up and learn to be stronger on our spiritual path.

Another thing to consider is Hermes' attribute of being "guide of dreams". Hermes is always moving. It is said that even when he sits, he is still moving. There is never a time when this god is not transitioning in some way. There is a reason that we call the process of dying *transitioning*. We are moving from one realm to another - from the physical plane to the spiritual plane. Dreams are a gateway to the spirit world, and it would make sense that as Hermes guides us through dreams while we are alive so, too, does he guide us to the ancestral lands when we die.

Charon

In Greek mythology, Charon is the divine ferryman who escorts the dead from the land of the living to the gates of Hades. He is the son of the great Titans Erebus and Nyx. Erebus means darkness and Nyx means night. So, Charon was birthed from the dark aspects of night. He was depicted by Virgil as a disheveled old man. In the *Aeneid Book VI*, it says:

A grim ferryman watches over the rivers and streams,
Charon, dreadful in his squalor, with a mass of unkempt
white hair straggling from his chin: flames glow in his eyes,
a dirty garment hangs, knotted from his shoulders.

He poles the boat and trims the sails himself,
and ferries the dead in his dark skiff,
old now, but a god's old age is fresh and green.

Once Hermes guides the spirits of the dead down into the Underworld, Charon takes them to the river Acheron. In Roman mythology the river is called Styx. Once the dead are delivered to the river, it is the ferryman, Charon, who is tasked to take them across to the gates of Hades. However, he does this for a price. In Greco-Roman funerary custom, a coin called an *obol* was placed in the mouth of the dead as payment to Charon. It was said that those who could not make the payment were left to wander the Underworld at the banks of the river for 100 years. Those unattended spirits were then under the care of Hekate, goddess of gates. Charon would also ferry the living across the river to the gates of Hades as long as they could make the payment. In modern times, Charon is sometimes portrayed as the Grim Reaper with his skeletal body, but the ancients did not see him like this. This portrayal has more to do with our modern association that all things "underworld" are all skulls and bones. He is a primordial being and is one of the Titans who were born when the Universe was new. As it is described in myth and lore, his nature is indifferent to the human race. Not only can he take the dead to the gates of Hades, he has the power to take the dead from Hades back to the river shores so they may once again walk among the living. One of the many benefits of working with Charon is that he is one of the great beings born at the beginning of the Universe. His energies are focused on taking the dead to the Gates of Hades and has many things to teach you about being a Psychopomp.

Anubis

Anubis is the jackal headed god whose primary purpose in ancient Egypt was to prepare the dead for their journey into the Egyptian Underworld, called the *Duat*. His name in Egypt was actually Anpu, but the Greeks called him Anubis. This is the name that our modern world commonly uses. Originally, Anubis was the ruler of the Underworld, but by the Middle Kingdom, this role was given to Osiris, the god of death and resurrection. After the Middle Kingdom, Anubis' role was changed from Underworld ruler to the god who mummified the body of Osiris after he was killed by the jealous god Set. From that time on, Anubis was known as the god of funeral rites and the one who weighs the heart of the deceased. I think it is interesting to note that the reason Anubis is depicted with a jackal or dog's head is because jackals were known to dig up the bones of shallow graves. To the Egyptian observer, this was a clear sign that the jackals were not causing harm to the graves, but rather were protecting the graves from robbers and so forth. This is how Anubis came to be known as the protector of tombs.

In Egyptian cosmology, when a person died, they had to endure many trials and guardians in the Underworld. If they were wealthy, they would be armed with magical spells from *The Book of Going Forth By Day* or commonly known as *The Egyptian Book of the Dead*. The spells helped the spirit of the dead journey through the treacherous Underworld until they were greeted by Anubis, who would then lead them to the Hall of Justice where they were awaited by 42 gods who questioned the deceased about how they lived their mortal life. Once this was done, Anubis would weigh the person's heart on the magical scales of truth against the feather of Ma'at. Ma'at translates to *truth*. The idea was that a lifetime of misdeeds would weigh down a person's heart and therefore would be heavier than the feather. If this was the case, then the spirit of person would be thrown into the pit of Ammit where they would be devoured. If the heart was lighter than the feather of truth, then they would be guided to the Land of the Ancestors. This made Anubis one of the most popular of the Egyptian deities, not just because he was the god of mummification, but because he was protector and guide of the dead.

Valkyries

The Valkyries are the warrior spirit women who take the chosen of the slain up to the Odin's great hall named Valhalla. It is in this great hall that the spirits of the slain will go to battle with each other by day and by night they will feast, drink, and make merry with Odin until they fight at the great battle Ragnarok. Valkyrie comes from the Old Norse word *valkyrja* and means "chooser of the slain". These spirits were seen as fierce warriors who would choose who on the battlefield would lose their lives and be taken up to feast in Odin's hall. Once the warrior dead resided in Valhalla, the Valkyries would serve them food and drink. Sometimes they were depicted as beautiful shield maidens who carried the dead to the heavens, while other times they were seen as warrior women who weaved the fate of death into a loom made from the intestines of the dead. In his book, *The Viking Spirit: An Introduction to Norse Mythology and Religion,* Daniel McCoy says:

> "...twelve Valkyries are seen prior to the Battle of Clontarf, sitting at a loom and weaving the tragic fate of the warriors. They use intestines for their thread, severed heads for weights, and swords and arrows for beaters, all the while chanting their intentions with ominous delight."

Valkyries were different from other guides of the dead because they did not guide all spirits to the afterlife. They chose only warriors for Odin's hall. Another characteristic that makes them unique is that in mythology, they would sometimes have sexual relationships with men. They would even help those in battle who they felt worthy of their divine power. These beings had the power to affect the fate of men in battle and by doing so, it would make sense that they could influence the outcome of the battle. Valkyries as psychopomps are immensely powerful allies and have a unique mystery of death, battle, and honor.

Gwyn Ap Nudd

Gwyn Ap Nudd (pronounced Gwen ap Neeth) is the Welsh god of Annwfn (pronounced Anoon) and can be found in faery mounds as well as mountains and hills. Annwfn is the Welsh Underworld and is the home of faeries as well as the dead. This is a place of beauty, rest, and rejuvenation for the weary spirit of the dead. There are many magical places in Annwyn that are represented by mystical castles. Each of these castles, or *Caer,* has a magical power and is home to some of the fey as well as the ancestors. Gwyn Ap Nudd is sometimes seen with antlers and at times has a bright or illuminating appearance. The name, Gwyn, itself translates as "white", "holy", or "fair". In Celtic, cosmology, a being or animal that is white or bright in appearance means that it is a spiritual being from the Otherworld. In many Celtic stories and lore, the faeries and the ancestors are sometimes found in the same place. This has led many observers to believe that the faeries are not Otherworldly beings, but rather the spirits of the dead. I have said many times before, that our ancestors and the fey are not the same being. However, I believe that upon death everyone has free will to go to wherever they chose at death. So, who's to say that those with a strong connection with the faeries do not chose to live with them after they have died. It is for these reasons, that Gwyn Ap Nudd is a god over both the dead and the faeries.

Gwyn Ap Nudd is the leader of the Welsh Wild Hunt. The Wild Hunt is a ghastly nightly procession that usually begins at Samhain tide and lasts until the bright days of the year come once again. He takes the Wild Hunt through the night skies of the darkening year and it is considered an omen of death should you see it with your own eyes, but it is said you can hear the shrieking of the spirits as they process through the night. As witches and magical people, we have the power to see the Wild Hunt as it soars by. We can also journey with them if we choose in the fetch form or astral body. We can even get a glimpse of who is destined to die if we look closely at who has joined the ghostly procession. Danu Forest, in her book *Gwyn Ap Nudd: Wild God of Faerie Guardian of Annwfn* says;

"The Wild Hunt functions as a vast energetic wave sweeping across the land clearing away the dead and any unwelcome spirits, although it is also a subject of fear as an example of chthonic forces literally upending the normal structure and riding either across the land or in the sky bringing change, retribution for misdeeds or general chaos to the mortal world."

Azrael - The Angel of Death

Azrael is the angel of death in Jewish and Islamic traditions. In these traditions, he is believed to reside in the third heaven. Azrael is a great archangel and is tasked with taking the spirit from the physical body and leading them to the afterlife. His name means "he who helps God". Azrael has at times been associated with the Grim Reaper and is sometimes depicted with a black hooded cloak and holding a scythe. Azrael in tradition was never seen this way. He was thought to be a kind and beautiful angel who had compassion for the dying. He is a great being who leads the spirit of the dead to the Land of the Ancestors. In some Jewish mysticism, he is seen as the personification of evil. I have to say this is the furthest thing of what Azrael really is. Many people fear dying and what is beyond death. They associate all things that cause death, be it violence, war, murder, starvation, disease, and so forth, on Azrael. These things are not brought upon by the angel Azrael. He does not cause someone to die, but rather, he is the gentle spirit who takes the spirit from their body into the spiritual world of the ancestors.

Azrael can be a wonderful help in your psychopomp work. Not only is he an angelic psychopomp, but he can teach you how to see the "big picture" of someone's death as well as the great mysteries associated with death itself. He is kind and patient, but he cannot be detoured from his obligation to take the spirits of the dead into the afterlife. I personally work with him in my psychopomp work and have him on my altar of death. For me, I have found that he is incredibly valuable with this type of spirit work.

Archangel Michael

The Archangel Michael is perhaps one of the most famous of all angels in the Judeo-Christian pantheon. His name means "Who is like God". He is said to be the most powerful angel and is often depicted carrying a flaming sword. Michael is the great angel who conquered Lucifer and helped God cast him down from heaven. Along with his powers to enforce God's will, Michael is also a divine psychopomp. In Catholicism, he comes to the dying and gives them one more chance to be saved by believing in God. Like, Azrael, he takes the spirit of the dead from the physical body and takes them to heaven where he places the spirit on the heavenly scales of justice to determine if their spirit should reside in heaven or hell.

Even though Michael is depicted as the warrior of God, he can also be kind. Just before death, Michael tries desperately to give the unsaved the last chance to redeem themselves and accept God/Jesus as their Lord and Savior so they can live eternally in heaven. This is an act of compassion for all human beings. I would like to take a moment to point out that this is biblical lore and mythology, and I have found that spiritual beings who are psychopomps are not interested in taking people to places like the Christian hell. Spirits who perform psychopomp work chose to do this work because they are kind and have a place in their hearts for those who are making the great journey into death. There are many witches, magicians, and Spirit Walkers who work with angels of all different types in their healing work. In my experience, angels are divine beings who serve the greater good of the Universe and do not necessarily serve only one faith. Their concern is the betterment of the Universe and the human race.

Baron Samedi and Manman Brijit

In Haitian Vodou there are spirits known as the Ghede. The Ghede are spirits of the dead who were either lost or forgotten by the community. They tend to frequent graveyards, but they can be found anywhere in the world. We tend to think of lost and forgotten spirits as melancholy, tormented, or brooding, but the Ghede are anything but. They reside very close to the living, enjoy making lewd sexual jokes, and they enjoy dancing among the people during ceremonies and parties. They are even known to help women become pregnant and aid the sick in healing. Baron Samedi and Manman Brijit are the leaders of the Ghede. They are the Lwa, pronounced LO-wa, meaning *spirit,* who gather the lost dead and lead them to the afterlife.

Baron Samedi, literally the Baron of Saturday, is dressed in a top hat and black suit, as if he were dressed for his own funeral. He sometimes wears sunglasses with one lens out so that he can see in both the physical world and the world of the dead. In art and media, he is often portrayed as a man with white make up or white powder on his face to represent the face of death itself. I often see him with a skull painted on his face. Manman Brijit is the wife of the Baron and helps him gather the dead to take to the afterlife. She is not afraid to say what is on her mind and uses profanity often. She also shows no shame about her sexuality and empowers her followers to do the same. Baron Samedi and Manman Brijit can be found either under the largest cross or the largest tree in the cemetery.

These deities may seem a bit chaotic at times, but it is important to remember that these beings give the forgotten and lost dead purpose in the afterlife. They remind both the dead and the living that there are joys in this world and the spirit world. Death is not to be treated as melancholy and sadness but rather a joyous occasion filled with dance, food, love, and joy.... and perhaps a little chaos from time to time.

Santa Muerte

Santa Muerte is a Mexican folk saint that has become increasingly popular in both Mexico and the United States. Her name translates to *Saint Death,* but she is known by other names such as "The Bony Lady", "Pretty Girl", and "Holy Death". The statues and art of this saint depict a skeletal figure who holds a scythe as well as a globe of the world. She is dressed in a hooded robe much like the Grim Reaper, but her robes are not just black. They can be found in many colors including red, gold, green, blue, purple, and white. She is often confused with the Grim Reaper. The Grim Reaper is an artistic expression of Death during the bubonic plague that killed millions of people during 14th century in Europe and has come to symbolize the Angel of Death in our modern times. Santa Muerte is not the Angel of Death, but rather the being of Death itself. In our Universe, since all things must eventually die, Santa Muerte has dominion over all things. It is sometimes said that she is second to only God.

It is believed by some scholars that Santa Muerte is an adaptation, or the spiritual evolution, of the Aztec goddess of the Underworld, Mictecacihuatl. The Aztecs believed that Mictecacihuatl took the spirits of the dead into the Underworld where they would await with her to be reborn into the next age. Santa Muerte has become very popular because not only does she have a great many powers, but she has no judgement or concern about the private affairs of humans. She is the energy of death itself and because of this she understands the triumphs and failings of all people. Through her, all people are equal because death is equal. All things must die, and the act of death has no judgement. Her followers consist of both the wealthy and poor, straight and LGTBQ, and criminals and model citizens alike. Santa Muerte has dominion over all things and she has many powers that she can grant those who ask for special requests of her. The colors of her robe have special significance. Each color represents the type of magick she is able to do for you:

White - Purification magick
Red - Love magick
Gold - Money Magick
Green - Justice and Court Case Magick
Blue - Social Relationships and Business Magick
Purple - Healing Magick
Black - Death, Curses, and Necromancy Magick

For the purposes of our psychopomp work, we will focus on the aspect of her that takes us into death and the afterlife. Santa Muerte, in her black-death aspect, has the power to take the spirit of the dead into the Land of the Ancestors. In his book *Devoted To Death: Santa Muerte The Skeleton Saint,* R. Andrew Chesnut says, "Santa Muerte is first and foremost an unofficial saint who heals, protects, and delivers devotees to their destination in the afterlife."

She is the compassionate skeletal being who has the power to heal as well as to give someone their last breath before taking them into the afterlife. She does this without judgment nor remorse. Santa Muerte also has the power to open the gates between this world and the world of the dead in order to help us take a lost spirit back home to their ancestral loved ones. With this in mind, she can also bring the spirits of the dead to us in order to speak to our loved ones in spirit. One thing to remember before connecting with Santa Muerte as a Psychopomp Teacher is that she prefers to have an altar all of her own and does not like to share space with any other deity or spirit. Some of her favorite offerings are tequila, tobacco smoke, and chocolate.

Ascended Ancestors

The Ascended Ancestors are our ancestors who have spiritually evolved to become divine and function in the role as spirit guide, guardian, teacher, and healer. The purpose of reincarnation is to give us many opportunities to spiritually evolve by creating multiple lifetimes that have life lessons. This allows us to have multiple life experiences. It is impossible for one life to teach us everything we need to know spiritually. In this philosophy each of us will eventually be able to progress on our great spiritual path until we are so evolved that we expand our consciousness and connect with the Universe very deeply. Once this occurs, we will be able to "ascend" our spirit and become divine ourselves. Once we are "godlike" we can take the lessons we have learned and help those on Earth walk the spiritual path they have chosen for themselves.

Ascended ancestors make wonderful Psychopomp Teachers because they know what it is like to be human. They once had human weaknesses, fears, and many other faults that make us human. They can teach us many things in our psychopomp work which include having compassion for the people we are working with. The ascended ancestors also have a deeper understanding for the work that we are doing and can teach us to have patience with ourselves.

Finding Your Psychopomp Teacher

For this technique you will be going on a Spirit Walk, a shamanic journey. You will be creating a sacred ceremony to find your

Pychopomp Teacher. By performing the ritual, you will place your mind, heart, and spirit in sacred space. This will allow your consciousness to open to the world of the spirits so that you can more easily connect to your teacher. For this ceremony, you will be journeying to the Underworld and the Land of the Ancestors and to find your Psychopomp Teacher.

To begin you will need to clean your magical space with a fumigation or smudge. You can use sage, mugwort, frankincense and myrrh, or any other herb in a fireproof vessel that makes you feel spiritual. You can light candles if you choose. I always light candles when I am doing any kind of spiritual work. You will also need to have an offering for the spirit. You can use bread, milk, wine, beer, mead, or food of some kind. If you prefer to journey with a drumbeat, you can do this as well. You can drum for yourself or easily find a drumming track on iTunes or Amazon. Another thing you can do to enhance your journey experience is to cover yourself using a special blanket or cloak. I like using a cloak because not only does it block out the senses for an effective journey, but it reminds of the sacred solemn nature of our psychopomp work.

1. Prepare your sacred space. Cleanse the space with a fumigation. Light your candles.
2. Take a few deep breaths and place yourself in a mental space of sacredness.
3. Pray to the spirits and ask that your Psychopomp Teacher come to you so that you may begin your path of healing the spirits of the dead.
4. If you choose to have music, turn it on or begin drumming.
5. Close your eyes and take a few more deep breaths. Know that you will be traveling into the Underworld to find your teacher. Relax your body, your mind, and your emotions.

6. Use a journeying technique of your choice and journey to the World Tree. Once there, state your intention again to find your Psychopomp Teacher, and travel down the roots of the great tree until you find yourself in the Underworld.

7. What part of the Underworld are you in? Are you in the Land of the Ancestors? Are you in a forest or garden? Allow the Underworld landscape to take shape as it will. Once there call again to you Psychopomp Teacher.

8. When your teacher appears to you, introduce yourself. Ask them who they are and spend some time getting to know the teacher. Ask them formally if they would be willing to be your Psychopomp Teacher and what types of offerings they prefer. Remember, after each teaching session and ceremony you will want to give them an offering of some kind.

9. Once you are finished, say your thanks and goodbyes, then come back to your physical body. Ground and center as needed.

10. Leave an offering for your teacher.

Working with Psychopomp Teachers

Once you have decided on which gods or spirits you would like to connect with in your psychopomp work, you will need to work with these beings several times a week. You can speak with them in a spirit journey or you can conjure them to your magical space by lighting your psychopomp altar and summoning the spirits to the physical plane. Personally, I use both of these techniques to learn from the spirits, but you can choose only one if you prefer. These beings will help you refine your skills as a healer to the spirits of the dead. For most of us magical folk, we enjoy having altars for our magical and healing work. In my temple space in my home, I have an altar set up that is dedicated to my Psychopomp Teachers. The teachers I chose are Azrael and Hekate. Even though they come from different pantheons, I have found that they work well together.

To set up a psychopomp altar, you will need to obtain statues or pictures of your chosen teachers. If you are using established gods or spirits, then it will be relatively easy to find statues. Doing an Amazon or Google search will yield good results. If you are working with Psychopomp Teachers who are not gods, you may either find an icon that represents them, or you may use a picture, drawing, or symbol to represent their energies on the altar. For example, you can use a feather, stone, crystal, or some other object that feels right to you. I have a candle for each of my teachers that I light to represent their spiritual presence as I perform my psychopomp work. You should have a small offering bowl for them as well. I also like incense on the altar but there is nothing that says you must have it if that is not to your taste. Personally, I like the esthetic of skulls and bones on the altar. However, I do use the skulls as magical tools in my magical work. When doing psychopomp work at hospices, hospitals, or someone's home, you do not need a psychopomp altar set up. The altar is for your spiritual development and to honor the spirits with whom you work.

Chapter 3

The Afterlife

We incarnate in the physical world so that we can spiritually evolve. From a spiritual standpoint, the earthly plane has the ability to accelerate the speed in which we are able to learn lessons that have a lasting effect upon our spirit. Have you heard the term, "I am a spiritual being having an earthly experience?" This is one of the mantras that I follow. We are all spiritual people, but as long as we are on the physical plane, we need to have experiences. I think that is what life is all about. It is about having experiences that shape our spirit. There are some religions that teach that suffering helps us spiritually evolve. This can be true, but suffering does not have to be the only way. Pain and suffering can shape our spirit to grow but can also shape our spirit to be closed off and unloving. In my experience and study of Spirit, the Universe cares less about suffering and more about creating an *experience* for us. I believe that experience is what shapes us. It is experience that helps us spiritually evolve. Pain and suffering are surely a part of life. But not the only part. Life can be joyful and pleasurable as well. What shapes our spirit is the ability to see connection and healing through all of our life experiences.

I do not believe that we are here in the physical plane for a time that is ordained by the Universe. The time we are incarnated in this life is based upon our capacity and willingness to learn spiritual lessons as well as to teach spiritual lessons to others. I have come to believe that part of our lessons on Earth is not only for us to learn, but for us to teach and heal others as well. As a healer, I truly believe that part of the reason we are in this physical life is to learn the spiritual lesson of healing others. Just to learn our spiritual lessons for our own sake is not enough. We have to take what we have learned and share it with those who need it. When I read the news from around the world, it is clear that the world needs healing in many different ways.

When the time has come and we have learned everything we can in this life and we have shared with others everything we are able to share, then our life upon the physical earth comes to an end. There are those who may live to a very old age while others die very young. There are many reasons for this. It is true that we may never know why people die when they do. Perhaps for some people we are not meant to know why they died when way they did. Other people die because they have done everything they were meant to do in this life and it time for them to transition to the next phase in their spiritual evolution and travel to the afterlife. Unfortunately, some people die because they have gotten so far off their spiritual path that they need to find healing in the spirit world. This is unfortunate, but we can see this in drug overdoses, gun violence, and reckless behavior.

How we live our lives can give us meaning. Also, how we face death can give us meaning. It has been said that those who have lived a full life face death with ease. This is because when a person has lived a full life, they understand that death is final experience of a life well lived. Those who have feared life and have avoided the many experiences that life has to offer may fear death. Perhaps this is because their whole life was lived in the fear of having valued experiences. So, when death approaches their life may feel unlived and they may not be ready to go into the next phase of their journey because something may feel undone. We all fear death in some way. The fear of death is built in our consciousness. We should fear death somewhat. That is what keeps us alive and keeps us from recklessly putting ourselves in harm's way. Just as our lives are sacred, our death is sacred as well. It is a spiritual transition to a place beyond the veil and into the spirit world. Some people call it the afterlife while others call it the realm of the ancestors.

No One Travels Alone

When the time of death is approaching, our physical body begins to lose its life force. Someone who is in the process of dying may begin to sleep a lot more or seem to be daydreaming. Oftentimes this is caused by medications that are given in order to alleviate pain. As the dying person's lifeforce begins to withdraw, they may find themselves speaking with people we cannot see. Many people who are close to death have seen the presence of relatives long dead and even seen beloved pets who have died many years before. For them, the veil between the worlds is becoming thinner and their ancestors are coming to them in order to give them comfort and reassurance. Those who do not understand the ways of Spirit may say that the dying are known to hallucinate, but in reality, they are seeing the spirits who are preparing them for the great journey ahead.

When we are born into the physical world there are a number of people in the delivery room. There are, of course, the mother, the doctors, and the nurses who are helping to facilitate the baby's birth. There are also sometimes other people in the delivery room. There is the father, other immediate family members, and sometimes close friends. To be born into this world is a community effort. Transitioning to the afterlife is similar to this. There are spiritual healing beings who will assist the dying. These beings can be gods and goddesses, angels, healing helpers, and spirit guides. As we said earlier, there are even pets who are excitedly anticipating the return of their companion. Just as our family welcomes us into the birth of the physical world, our ancestors welcome us into the transition into the afterlife.

As physical death approaches, there is an energetic reverberation that extends throughout the energy worlds. Even before the dying know it themselves, the ancestors can feel when one of their relatives and friends are approaching the threshold between life and death. Our ancestors are linked to us energetically. The same blood that flowed through their veins flows through our veins. The history of our ancestors can be found in our physical genetics. Using this same philosophy, our ancestors are energetically connected to us through every single cell that we have in our bodies. They will always be a part of us, and we will always be a part of them. We are connected through time and space. Through this connection, they will know when it is time to welcome us home. Our ancestors and healing spirits are preparing us for the great transition into the afterlife by preparing our energy body as well as our consciousness for what lies beyond the veil between this life and the next.

When the time comes for us to leave our body, all brain function will stop. The body will be clinically dead, and our astral spiritual body will be released from the physical form. Our spirit will be free from the physical plane so that we may make the journey into the Land of the Ancestors. During this process, the ancestors and healing spirits will fill the room with a great healing energy. Some call this energy love. Others call this energy Spirit. This energy will give the transitioning person comfort and a sense of trust to go with the spirits through the portal into the afterlife. The ancestors will walk gently with them, comforting them along the way. The transitioning person is not alone. They are taken care of and they are loved.

Welcome Home

Once the transitioning person arrives in the Land of the Ancestors there is big welcoming for them. All their ancestors who are still in the ancestral lands gather to welcome their family member home. The person is surrounded by family and friends and are encompassed with love. They are home. I am betting that you are wondering why I call the Land of the Ancestors home. Well, there are few reasons for this. The first reason is that our physical world and our time here is only temporary. Many spiritual traditions believe that the spirit world was created to be a permanent place while the physical world is only temporary. Science has proven this to be true. Astrophysics teaches that the Universe as we know it will either burn out, leaving a cold shell where life once lived, or it will crash into itself trying to return to its source. Either way, at some point, the physical Universe will cease to exist, but the spiritual Universe will continue. Another reason I call the Land of the Ancestors home is because home is where our loved ones are. Home is where our family is as well as those friends and pets that we call family.

The Land of the Ancestors is not the heaven that is spoken about in any patriarchal religion. The spirit world is not as black and white as that. There are many different worlds or perhaps a better way to put it is that there are many dimensions to the afterlife. There is no hell or place of punishment, but there is a shadowland which we will talk about at the end of this chapter. What dogmatic religions fail to understand is that human beings are complicated spiritual creatures that have complicated spirits. People are complicated and so are the spirit worlds. The Universe understands that people learn in many different ways and express both joy and sorrow in many different ways. There is no punishment for a "sin" that some man came up with thousands of years ago. There is only our willingness to learn from our mistakes and continue to walk upon the path of spiritual evolution.

To understand what the afterlife is like we must take a moment and discuss the nature and magick of our consciousness. We hear all the time that the power of our mind has the ability to do anything. It can not only cast spells and do magick, but it can quite literally shape the physical world around us. How is it able to do that? The mind is a powerful energy force that is not confined to physical barriers. We know this because with our mind we are able to astral project and reach out to other minds with telepathy. We can do this because the mind defies the laws of the physical world set with its physical limitations. It is able to shape our environment here on Earth because we are able to link with the creative force of the Universal consciousness and create change in our world. Granted, sometimes this takes a while to accomplish because physical changes need to occur to make a solid change. Now, imagine you did not have the confines of the physical laws of nature. Imagine that your mind was able to connect to the creative force of the Universe. Instead of waiting until physical things manifest in your environment you can instantly change your surroundings because you do not have the physical barriers of the physical plane. This would mean that you could shape any energetic force in accordance to your Will at the speed of thought.

You will be able to create your environment in your afterlife in any way you like. The weather, if you want to call it that, is always warm and gentle and you have no need for shelter, but if you would like a residence all your own you could create your own home by thinking it. You can also create any environment that you like. If you wanted it to snow because you enjoyed skiing, then all you would have to do is think it and it would be so. The ancestors will often gather in familiar communities and will have agreed upon how their environment will look. What usually happens is that a group of people from the same part of the world will imagine that their environment would manifest in a certain way. For example, if you lived in the mountains than your environment would be mountainous. If you lived in a tropical climate then your environment would be tropical. No matter what kind of landscapes you encounter in the afterlife they are exceptionally beautiful. In his book, *The Afterlife Unveiled: What 'the Dead' Tell Us About Their World*, Stafford Betty relates to us the description of the afterlife from the spirit of a man who died in 1886 "...Summerland is enchantingly beautiful. Gorgeous trees and flowers, shady glades and rushing streams, towering mountains and sparkling lakes, striking land features and charming little villages, vast oceans with islands, and large cities - all of these are here."

Helper Spirits

There are many helper spirits that will aid the person while they are in the Land of the Ancestors. Some traditions have called them guardian angels, spirit guides, and many other names. I prefer to call them helper spirits because they act as helpers and teachers to the person who has recently arrived in the afterlife. Someone's ancestors can certainly be helper spirits, but family is still family and even ancestors with the best intentions will seek to help them through the viewpoint of a caring family member. The helper spirit can be any type of being who seeks to "walk" the new spirit through the different aspects of the afterlife. When a person first arrives in the afterlife they are welcomed by their ancestors and they are taken care of and made sure that they understand that they are loved. A helper spirit makes themselves available for any questions or concerns that the person may have during their first moments in the spirit world.

Helper spirits are great teachers and spiritual counselors. They will answer any and all questions the person may have. Just imagine for a moment that your life on the physical earth has ended and you are now in the afterlife. Wouldn't you have questions? The helper will help them understand the world that they are now in. They will help ease their anxieties and any fears that they may have. For some people, they may have expected to end up in a place of angels playing harps and dancing on clouds. This is definitely not what the afterlife looks like and many religious people who never questioned their own religion may be confused that they did not end up in a biblical heaven. The same can be said for people who led a troubled life on the physical plane and thought that they may end up in hell or purgatory at best. Helper spirits reassure the new spirit that the afterlife has nothing to with rewards or punishments but rather a place of sanctuary and healing.

Those of us who have studied magick and energy work are very aware of how we can manipulate energy and journey anywhere in the three shamanic worlds. Most people do not know anything about this. They may have vaguely heard about it but never learned about it during their lifetime, the helper spirit will teach them how to do these things. For the record, the ancestors are not bound to the Land of the Ancestors, they have free reign to go anywhere in the Universe that they choose. However, just as many people do not travel very far away from their homes in life, they may not travel very far from the ancestral lands in spirit.

Anything that someone may need help with, the helper spirit will gladly guide them through the areas of concern they may have. There are many things they need to learn and understand while they are there. For some, the transition is very smooth, and the person may only need a little guidance here and there. But for others, the transition may seem confusing and they may need more help than others. The helper spirits are happy to help anyone no matter where they are on their spiritual path and their ability to navigate through the otherworlds. No one is left alone during their transition from the physical plane to the world of the spirits.

Life Review

Once the person has acclimated to the new surroundings, it is important that they do a life review. A life review is an opportunity for someone to go over their life in great detail. It is here that they go over every action and inaction that they did, or did not do, in life. It is important to understand that there is no sin in the Universe. The Universe has more patience with us than we can sometimes understand. In life, we are spiritual beings living an earthly existence meant to live life to the fullest we can. We are not perfect. I believe that we are perfect in our imperfections. It is our imperfect design that allows us to evolve.

The Universe cares less about our actions and more about our ability to learn the lessons that are presented to us during our lives rather than if we did things the "right" or the "wrong" way. Right and wrong are judgements that the human race places upon itself to regulate behavior. As children we are taught right and wrong from our parents, teachers, and other adults because we have not yet gained the capacity to understand the fullness of our actions. It is hopeful that as we grow up, we can make our own decisions on how we choose to interact with the world. Not everyone has this ability or chooses not to have it. These people need someone to hold them accountable for their actions. Governments and religions tell people what they should and should not do. They establish laws of the land or of god that define the boundaries that should not be crossed in order to have a civilized life. In my opinion, we should not need a rule or a law to tell us that we should not cause harm to people. It seems strange to me that some people need to be told "do not kill". I believe that rules and laws do not make someone a good person. Choosing to help people, or at the very least to cause no harm, should come from your heart and not a law.

An important part of the life review is our capacity to love. Being able to love and to love deeply is probably one of the hardest lessons we have in our human lives. Loving people is hard, especially unconditional love. To love others can be particularly challenging and to allow others to love us can be even more challenging. We are complicated beings and our emotions are equally as complicated. The life review reminds us of all the times we were successful in loving someone truly and wholly. It can also remind us when we did not live up to our potential and we did not love as we should have or even could have. For many of us, we get in our own way when it comes to giving and receiving love. Our life review on love focuses on how we affected the lives of others. Are we creating an environment that is joyful and healing or are we creating an environment of neglect and mistrust? We are incarnated on the physical plane to love and heal others. How we accomplish this is completely up to us and healing can take a myriad of different forms. Life is multifaceted and each of us is tasked with discovering how we can love and help others.

During our life review if we discover that we have not lived up to our full potential or have outright failed, there is no punishment. That does not mean that in life you can harm people and do what you please and be selfish. The helping spirits help you understand how and why you were not able to help others. Remember, the Universe is not judging you, the Universe wants you to be the best version of yourself you can be. As one person spiritually evolves, so does the rest of the Universe. We are all connected. Our successes affect the cosmic web just as our failures affect the cosmic web. The Universe is spiritually invested in the development of each of us. No one is left behind.

From one Spiritual Dimension to Another

The afterlife is more complex than just a beautiful place to rest. It can certainly be a magical place where we have the opportunity to heal and renew our spirit from the hard work we endured in the physical plane, but it is so much more. The afterlife has other planes of existence, or dimensions for the lack of a better term. Upon death, your spirit vibrates at a certain spiritual level. When you arrive at the Land of the Ancestors, your spiritual vibration will find itself on the plane of existence that is congruent with the vibration of your spirit. Again, this is not a judgement. Think of it akin to a student testing out of school grades and being elevated to the next level. The reason for this is that, as we said before, no one is left behind, and each spirit will receive the care and healing they need in accordance to their spiritual level. I do not think one spiritual level is better or worse than another. It is just where we are in our spiritual evolution.

Let us take a moment to examine the different parts of the

afterlife. The first level of the afterlife is very similar to the physical world we live in now. There is not much difference other than the fact that you are not bound to the laws of the physical plane. You can never fall and hurt yourself and you can appear anywhere with just a thought. This plane has many of the pleasures of Earth such as food, sex, sports, games, drinking and many other things. This is not such a bad place! This plane helps the new spirit acclimate to their current condition as they heal and rejuvenate after a life lived on the physical plane. Another purpose is to give the new spirit comfort as they are adjusting to the new circumstance of the amazing journey that is ahead of them. This is not considered a bad place by any means. This plane is inhabited by spirits of the dead who may not have had a spiritual life and it would be overwhelming for them to be immediately placed in the higher planes. The Universe seeks to help each of us and is patient enough with us to understand sometimes the spirit may need to take baby steps on their spiritual path of evolution. During a person's time on various planes of the afterlife, healing spirits and the ancestors help them learn spiritual lessons that will help them progress through them.

The next plane is where most people find themselves when they arrive in the spirit world. I call this place the Land of the Ancestors. This is the beautiful, dreamlike, place that was described earlier in the chapter. This world is a place of vivid colors, wonderful landscapes, and many villages and cities where the ancestors reside and we are reunited with our loved ones. The Land of the Ancestors is a place where the ancestors can find rest, healing, and rejuvenate from the hard work of a physical existence. As we are well aware, the physical world has many joys and triumphs, but it also has many hardships, sadness, pain, and suffering. The Land of the Ancestors allows us a time to heal from the sorrow and pain that we endured in life. The helper and healing spirits will take great care in helping us understand our hardships and helping us heal. There are many places here where we can rest our weary spirits and find peace and understanding. In this plane, the world of magick and joy are intertwined. There are many places where people can learn anything they would like and love and beauty are celebrated. The ancestors may spend the majority of their time in the afterlife here. They can decide to reincarnate back on the physical plane, or they may progress up to the higher realms.

The next plane is the place where the spirit can evolve into an ancestral guide, spiritual teacher, or spirit guide for humans on the physical plane. Not everyone wishes to be a spirit guide, but it is in this plane of the afterlife where a person has spiritually evolved to a place where they begin to understand the deeper mysteries of the Universe. It is in this wondrous plane that is inhabited by what are called "higher beings". These beings consist of the helping spirits mentioned at the beginning of the chapter. These beings may or may not be human and they seek to teach and educate humans. These ancestors have evolved to such a state of joy and understanding that they wish others to learn to share their understanding of the Universe. The beings in this plane understand human faults and know that it is our faults that make us perfect in our own way. It is at this level of the afterlife that the ancestors have grown in consciousness to discover that the greatest joy in the Universe is to serve others and to support them upon their path. The landscape in this world is more abstract in appearance because the energy is more refined and closer to the Spiritual Plane than the lower planes. These planes are not better or worse than another, it is simply the level where the spirit resonates with the most.

The highest plane is the dimension that resonates with divine beings. Many magical and pagan traditions describe how our goal is to discover the divine within and to connect with the Universe on a "higher" level. Once a person spiritually evolves to this plane, they are divine in their own right. At this level of spiritual consciousness, they may become what is known as an ascended ancestor. These are people who have connected to a high level of divine expression. They may choose to dwell with other divine spirits or they may continue their path as teachers and guides only at this higher level. Ascended ancestors seek to help the Universe evolve even further on its path. Sometimes they may teach and guide as great spiritual beings or they may reincarnate on Earth as great teachers such as Martin Luther King Jr., Buddha, Rumi, and many others. This is the place found in the creative force of the myth and magick of the Universe. The energy is very abstract here, but for the living Spirit Walkers and witches who travel here in spirit it can be shaped by our thoughts and imaginations. We can commune with many divine beings at this level of spirit. It is easier for deities to travel down to the lower planes than it is for people who are in the lower planes to rise up. Yet, as magical people, we have the ability to journey into any of the planes. From a point of view of the Three Worlds, you could say that this is a part of the Underworld that blends with the Upperworld.

Journey to The Land of the Ancestors

In your work as a psychopomp we will need to be able to navigate the Land of the Ancestors. You will encounter many spirits who are earthbound and are unable to make the journey to be reunited with their ancestors. It will be up to us to escort these spirits to a place in the afterlife where they can find the healing that they need to continue on their spiritual path. To be able to guide the spirits is a sacred duty that few healers and Spirit Walkers will be able to do. In order for us to do this sacred work we must be familiar with the various levels of the ancestral lands. You will not be left alone on your journey. Your Psychopomp Teacher will go alongside you and guide you along the way. In this next exercise you will explore the Land of the Ancestors with the help of your Psychopomp Teacher.

1. You may sit or lie down for this exercise. If you like, you may play music and light incense. Any incense that makes you feel otherworldly and magical with do.

2. Take a few deep breaths and place yourself in light trance. Focus on the work that is to be done at this time.

3. State aloud your purpose to the spirits. You should speak from your heart, but you can say something like, **"I seek to journey to the Land of the Ancestors with my Psychopomp Teacher in order to learn to navigate this magical land."**

4. Close your eyes and visualize your Psychopomp Teacher standing before you. Ask them to guide you through the Land of the Ancestors.

5. Visualize a portal to the afterlife opening in your magical space. Your Psychopomp Teacher will guide you into the portal.

6. Your first encounter will be with the first level of the afterlife. This is the level that resembles the physical plane almost exactly. The spirits you will encounter here are the people who were attached to the materialistic ideas of the physical plane. We are not trying to help anyone evolve further at this time. We are only here to explore and observe. Spend some time in this world exploring your surroundings. Be sure to allow your Psychopomp Teacher to guide you. Take heed of any advice your Teacher may give you.

7. When you are ready, return to through the portal back to the physical world. Take a few breaths and bring yourself back to your everyday consciousness.

8. It is very important that you keep a journal of your experiences in the Land of the Ancestors. With your many journeys to the afterlife, you will have numerous journal logs that will help you learn to navigate these otherworldly places.

I recommend journeying with your Psychopomp Teacher to each of the ancestral lands three to five times before moving on to journeying to the shadowlands. Make sure you visit the first world of the afterlife, then the beautiful Lands of the Ancestors, then the place of spirit guides and helping spirits, and finally the world of the divine beings and Ascended Ancestors. Make sure you take several journeys to each of these magical places of the afterlife. With each journey, you will learn something new and have a deeper understanding of these worlds.

Shadowlands

In pagan and Witchcraft cosmology, there is no hell. There is no place where a wrathful god sends people into a lake of fire because they displeased him, or they did not believe in him or his teachings. Pagans and witches understand that these are myths created by people who sought to convert and control people through the fear of eternal punishment. We know that the afterlife is made up of energy and it is through our consciousness that we are able to shape the energy into an afterlife of our choosing. The common person does not realize how much power their mind actually has. Many people do not understand that, even in the physical world, they create their own world with their thoughts, emotions, actions, and deeds. The world they live in has been masterminded by their own consciousness. This is even more true for the afterlife.

As spiritual people, we try to understand ourselves as best as we are able. We try to understand our shadow selves and make the effort to work on our failings. Let us take a moment to look at what the shadow self is according to psychology. The shadow self is the part of our subconscious mind where we store repressed thoughts, beliefs, emotions, and desires. It is also what we deem for ourselves to be bad or undesirable in accordance to our own boundaries and belief structure. In other words, if we do not like something about our nature, we have a tendency to push it to the back of our minds and pretend it does not exist. As we know, when we do this, it will eventually creep back up on us when we least expect it. Now, let us take this philosophy and apply it to a person who does not see bad and unethical behavior as troublesome. They may repress these thoughts and emotions to their subconscious mind. We know that our thoughts and emotions have power. On top of all this, the person may have addictions, negative emotions, and actions that have caused harm to others. Imagine for a moment this person has died. Between their repressed shadow selves and their bad behavior causing their spirit to vibrate on a lower frequency, they may very well create for themselves a shadowland.

The shadowlands are a place that are dark and sometimes covered with fog. It is where the dead find themselves because the frequency of this land is congruent with the frequency of the spirit who dwells there. I want to make it crystal clear that this is not a punishment by any means. No god or angel put these spirits here. They placed themselves here. The spirits who are here were focused on negative energies in life and chose not to walk a path of kindness to others. The Universe is designed in such a way that there are many opportunities in our lives to help others in some way. This is what being of service means. It means to help others when we can. When we harm people instead of helping them our energy frequency becomes lower and attracts other lower energies. When a person enters the afterlife, their spirit will gravitate to the world whose frequency is in congruence with the frequency of the person.

As with the other spiritual dimensions of the afterlife, those people in the shadowlands have the opportunity to spiritually evolve. No one is left alone. Even the spirits of the dead who have a low vibration will have an opportunity to get out of their situation. The helping spirits and Ascended Ancestors will try to teach and help them the best they can to spiritually wake up and see that there are higher lands in the afterlife. Once they are able to raise their spiritual vibration, they will be able to leave the shadowlands. Remember, no one is forced into the shadowlands. They go there under their own volition, but most are unaware that they have placed themselves there. In order to evolve past this world, they simply have to "wake up" and understand what is happening to them. In his book *The Place We Call Home: Exploring The Soul's Existence After Death,* Robert J. Grant says:

"The free will every human being possesses in life continues after death. Only when the soul relinquishes its hold upon malice, hate, vengeance, and the things of the material world in order to embrace the light can the greater light come in. How quickly the process of leaving behind the material thoughts and desires after death goes is very much dependent upon how much spiritual consciousness is cultivated during the life on earth."

Psychopomp in the Shadowlands

All is not without hope in the shadowlands. There are many higher beings such as helper spirits and spirits guides who wish to help those people who have found themselves in the place of darkness and fog. The people who dwell in the shadowlands have not raised their hearts and mind enough to see that they can easily get out of this gloomy place. You may be asking yourself, "Why don't they just leave?" We have all seen people who get caught up in their own failings and life situation and have convinced themselves that there is no other way. That this is the life they have, and there is no getting out of it. The same can be said for people in the shadowlands who refuse to see that there is a better afterlife of joy waiting for them. Some people may think that they deserve to be in the shadowlands, while others are so preoccupied with their obsessions that they do not realize they can look to something more outside of themselves.

Along with the helper spirits and spirit guides, human psychopomps will travel to the shadowlands in order to help the dead see beyond the borders of the shadowland. They will guide those spirits out of their self-made misery in order to transition to the Land of the Ancestors so that they receive the healing they need to start walking upon their own spiritual path to a higher consciousness. As we are learning to be psychopomps, we will, at times, need to help the spirits who have lost themselves in the shadowlands. Our psychopomp teachers can help and guide you in this process. During our healing journey to help the shadowlands, we cannot force anyone to leave. They will leave when they are ready. Even if we did force someone to leave the dark places, they would find themselves back there because they were not ready.

It can be challenging to convince a person they would find more joy if they were to journey to the Land of the Ancestors. The first thing I do, is look for a spirit that is very close to opening their hearts to see the higher realms. I will go to them and speak with them further. Each person is different and the reasons they are in the shadowland are also different. Some people may be there because of crimes they committed in life. Other people may be there because they chose not to care about anyone but themselves and closed their hearts to love. Sometimes people are in the shadowland because they believed the lies that said that they deserved to be in a bad place because they were different. To me, this is the saddest reason of all. These poor people were convinced that because they committed some "sin" they deserved to be unhappy in the afterlife. As psychopomps, it is one of our responsibilities to explain to those in the shadowland that this is a temporary place and they can find the healing that they need in the higher realm of the Land of the Ancestors.

Psychopomp Journey to the Shadowlands

Just as you did with journeying to the Land of the Ancestors, you will need to journey with your Psychopomp Teacher to the Shadowlands. Our work as psychopomp will sometimes lead us to these dark and desolate places. It can be challenging to see the spirits of these people because they do not understand where they are or why they are there. Upon observation, it appears that the spirits here have forgotten what beauty and hope look like. Many of them are convinced they are happy here or have convinced themselves that there are no other places besides the Shadowlands. These are people who in life were preoccupied with unethical, addictive, obsessive, and destructive behaviors. Just as with living people who have these problems, the spirits of the dead are even more stubborn and focus on their dark feelings and do not see anything but these feelings.

The Psychopomp Teacher will train you how to deal with the spirits here and how to teach them that there are better worlds in the afterlife. It can feel very much like the spirits here have their focus on the dark ground and do not look up to see the healing energy of hope and light. They do not realize that they are not confined here. They are free to leave this place whenever they so choose. The trick is getting the spirits to understand this. During your first journeys to the Shadowlands, it is very important that you just observe your Psychopomp Teacher and do not engage the spirits. Allow your Psychopomp Teacher to guide you every step of the way. They will teach you how to handle yourself, what to say and not say, and what energy work to do if it is needed. Take all the time you need with this part of the psychopomp training. There is no need to rush.

1. You may sit or lie down for this exercise. If you like, play music and light incense. Any incense that makes you feel otherworldly and magical with do.
2. Take a few deep breaths and place yourself in light

trance. Focus on the work that is to be done at this time.

3. State aloud your purpose to the spirits. You should speak from your heart, but you can say something like, **"I seek to journey to the Shadowlands with my Psychopomp Teacher in order to learn to further my psychopomp training."**

4. Close your eyes and visualize your Psychopomp Teacher standing before you. Ask them to guide you through the Shadowlands.

5. Visualize a portal to the afterlife opening in your magical space. Your Psychopomp Teacher will guide you into the portal.

6. As you come through the other side of the portal you will be with your Psychopomp Teacher in the Shadowlands. You are to simply observe until your teacher tells you that you are ready. Your teacher will do all the psychopomp work at this time.

7. When you are ready, follow your Psychopomp Teacher back through the portal and back to your magical space.

8. Ask your teacher to place magical wards (symbols) in your home so no spirit may accidentally follow you back home. You may also ask your gods, guides, and ancestors to remove any spirits who may have followed you back. A quick note: normally spirits in the Shadowlands do not follow you back home. This is because your energy is a high vibration and they do not like it. It is why they are in the shadowlands in the first place. They are also too preoccupied with their own self-made drama to pay attention to higher beings such as you or your Psychopomp Teacher.

9. Bring yourself back to waking consciousness. Center and ground as needed and journal your teachings and experience.

Chapter 4

Spirit Communication

Spirit communication is perhaps the most important part of being a psychopomp. We can have the ability to conjure spirits, open portals into the Underworld, and send healing energy, but communicating with the spirits is where the real magick and healing is. Our job as a psychopomp is primarily that of a healer. In our healing work with the spirits, the most important aspect of it is talking with them and allowing them the opportunity to be heard. In this regard, our role is that of a spiritual counselor. In addition to this, we must be able to decipher the energies that are surrounding the residence of the spirit as well as the spirit themselves. We will need to use our psychic abilities to be able to read the energies of the spirit so that we can better understand the entirety of the circumstances surrounding the spirit and the life and death that they have lived.

In many books on spirit work, they do not give much detail on how to actually communicate with spirits, let alone see the spirits that we are working with. Many times, authors assume that if you are working with the spirits that you already know how. Some authors will tell the student to go find a teacher before you do any spirit work. I have also found that some authors are hesitant to teach readers how to see spirits. They fear that it would reflect poorly on them if the student is not disciplined enough to do the work or may not have the "talent" to see the spirits. If you have read any of my books, you will have seen that I do not shy away from teaching advanced magical work. I am not a fan of gatekeeping; and I think every person should take responsibility for their own actions. I have found that when the magical student is ready, they will be able to do advanced magical work. Another thing I want to talk about is talent. We all have the ability to work with the spirits. We all have psychic ability. All of us. Some people may pick up psychic techniques faster than others, but I do not believe that makes them a better psychic or spirit communicator in the long run. What makes someone successful at psychic skills is being disciplined and practicing the techniques daily.

Many schoolteachers will tell you that each student learns differently and judging someone's learning ability by the same standard tests does the student a disservice. Some students catch on to mathematical formulas quicker than others, while another student can look at a machine for the first time and tell you exactly how it works by looking inside. My brother is a good example. In school, he was never the student who excelled in reading or math, but from a very young age he was able to take a broken machine apart, fix it, and put it back together again. When I had my first car, used of course, I had him do all the repairs on it and he was not even old enough to drive. That is just how his brain works. Even though he gravitated towards fixing machines and cars at a very young age, that does not mean that someone in their 20's, 30's, or even 70's cannot learn to fix a machine just as well as him. It may take a lot more practice and discipline, but it can be done and done well. The reason I bring this up, is because there are some magical students who hear how one person can see spirits their whole life, or was an amazing tarot reader from the age of five, and they believe that they will never be as good at being psychic or seeing spirits. From my years of teaching magical students I have found that magical talent can get you on the path, but it is discipline and determination that will help you become a powerful witch or psychic.

When it comes to psychic ability, not everyone learns the same way nor has the same aptitude for a particular psychic skill. We are all "wired" differently. Because we have different thought patterns, points of view, zodiac signs, cultural upbringings, and likes and dislikes, we will naturally gravitate towards certain skills while having to work hard at others. This does not mean you will have to just be "not very good" at something. This means that for certain psychic abilities you will have to work harder while sharpening other skills that come easy to you. When I was little, my mom's aunt used to tell us stories about Ouija boards, ghosts, hauntings and so forth. These stories of speaking with ghosts sounded like the coolest thing in the world. I could not wait to get a Ouija board and talk to ghosts. Also, in my family dreams were believed to be premonitions into the future. So, we were exposed to these things from an early age. As I grew older, I found that I was able to summon and send energy very well. Because I am a strong energy worker, my ability to work with dreams and see the future became weaker. It was not until I got formal magical training that I was able to cultivate *both* skills.

In this chapter, I will teach you the skills and exercises needed in order to work with spirits effectively in our psychopomp work. One of the things I want you to keep in mind is that all of us have to practice magical and psychic techniques. Even those of us who have been practicing magick and psychic skills for many years. Just as with any sort of exercise, if you have not practiced in a long time you will be a bit rusty. Some of the techniques will be easy for you while others will be more challenging. Try to work through each of the techniques with a beginner's mind and not have judgement upon yourself if you are having trouble with one of the techniques. When I was first learning how to scry, it took me a while to be able to see the images in the scrying device well. It was a bit frustrating because I could read the tarot and cast spells very well but seeing the images in the magick mirror or scrying bowl was harder for me. I decided to really practice it every single day until I became a master at it. Eventually, I was able to see into a crystal ball or magick mirror as well as the most experienced witch. When we have to spend extra time with a technique, it is not a reflection of how experienced you are as a witch or psychic. It simply means this is yet another thing you must master with diligence and practice. Remember, even the best magicians must practice every day. This is what makes them the best.

Belief

One of the most important parts of magick and psychic ability is to simply believe that it is real. It is equally important that you BELIEVE that you have the power to perform these wonderful things. As a teacher and spiritual leader, I can tell immediately who does not believe in magick within any group I work. When someone does not believe in magick or psychic powers, it feels to me like there is a hole sucking out the energy of the space where the energy should be free flowing. In large groups, a non-believer is not that important because the other attendees who do believe in the power overpowers the one who does not. In smaller groups, it causes the other people to have to work harder than they should to conjure the magical power.

Your mind is immensely powerful and it can affect the flow of energies in your body as well as affect the psychic energy in any room you are in. Energy is meant to flow freely. Everything from our body's energy to an electrical current is meant to flow with ease. If there is a short in the wires or something blocks the flow of the energy, then it will stop in its tracks. When someone does not believe in psychic power it is essentially creating an energy block in the chakras and the meridians in the energy body of the nonbeliever. It also causes the aura of the person to shrink so the energy flow is impeded even further. It is interesting to me that whatever you believe or do not believe becomes a self-fulfilling prophecy. You have the ability to create your own world or become a prisoner of it. Yes, your mind is that powerful.

It is normal for someone, even skilled practitioners, to second guess their psychic ability. Many of us are brought up in

Christian households or families who do not believe in magick and psychic power. We are sometimes taught from an early age that what we think is magick is just coincidence or simply part of our imagination. In my magical training, I remember my teachers saying "suspend disbelief during magical practice or a ritual". Essentially, if you are having doubts of what is real or unreal, for the time being just have an open mind and act as if it is real. By doing this, you will keep our energies flowing which will allow your psychic powers to come through. When you are able to achieve results, you will gain more confidence in your abilities.

Meditation-Tuning into the Energies

Many students come to me for training because they want to learn to advance their skills with magick. Some want to conjure the gods and angels while others seek to summon the dead. I have some students who want to become Spirit Walkers who look for lost soul fragments to heal the sick. The one magical technique that I make sure all of them are able to master is meditation. When I present this to my students, they often react with an eye roll. The world meditation is often thought of as New Age nonsense that is for people trying to relax and is taught in wellness centers. Well, it sure is taught in New Age practices, but meditation is another powerful technique that must be mastered in order to be able to speak with the spirits. In order for you to learn how to communicate with spirits you must be able to place your mind in an altered state of consciousness. Meditation is one of the best and simplest ways to achieve an altered state. Meditation in order to tune in to energy is often overlooked but yet is one of the best ways to communicate with the spirits.

There are three types of meditation that I use often for myself as well my students. The first and perhaps the easiest for some people is guided visualization. I often use guided visualization meditation when I am helping people take their first journeys as a Spirit Walker in the Three Worlds. This helps people get their bearings when they are first exploring the spiritual realms. Once the student becomes comfortable with guided meditation, I will help them add other magical techniques during their visualizations. Another meditation technique is to empty the mind as best as possible. I call it "seeing black". In other words, you are not visualizing anything. Instead, you are decluttering your mind and turning off all thoughts in order to connect to the Universe. For many practitioners, they not only receive many health benefits, but are able to connect to the Universe so that they may speed the process of their spiritual evolution. During this type of meditation, it is common to receive wisdom and insights that help on their spiritual path. The last form of meditation that I use is to connect to energies and spirits. During this form of meditation, you will be able to clear your mind and connect to your psychic powers and forces of energies, as well as connect to the spirits.

This meditation technique is very simple. But do not let the simplicity of it fool you, it will be the most common tool in your magical toolbox.

1. Sit comfortably in a chair, couch, or on the floor.
2. I like to light a candle and incense. You can do this or simply meditate without it. I have found when you create sacred space, your meditations become more successful.
3. Take a few deep breaths and relax your mind, relax your emotions, and relax your body as best you can.
4. Your goal is to "tune in" to the Universe for wisdom, insight, and gnosis.
5. Open your heart chakra and your brow chakra. The idea here is to feel and see the energies in your mind. Imagine that your psychic mind (brow chakra) and your emotions (heart chakra) are connecting to the Universe.

It may help to visualize these chakras opening up like a flower to receive the Universal energies.

6. Bring to mind the cosmos, the galaxies, and all of creation. Do not try to think about it too hard or "figure it out". Just connect. The Universe will provide you with the insight you need.

7. Quiet your thoughts as much as possible and just allow the energies to appear as they will without forcing them. A helpful hint is to try your best not to judge what you are doing. Open your mind and be open to the experience.

8. What do you see in your mind? What do you hear? How do you feel? Try your best to have non-judgment about your meditation experience.

9. Sometimes wisdom and gnosis come to you as a "knowing". You may not see much, but you just know it's something from the Universe.

10. Journal your experience.

The Sphere of Sensation

The Sphere of sensation is your psychic awareness that surrounds your physical body. It is connected to the aura but is thought to be separate from the aura itself. To clarify, the energy of the aura is created by the chakras and the life force of the human body while the Sphere of Sensation is a sphere of magical or psychic consciousness, called the Spirit Consciousness by The Golden Dawn, created by the psychic output of the mind and to some extent the body. I find it interesting that the Sphere of Sensation is not traditionally found in Kabbalistic theory but was taught in The Golden Dawn's magical theory. In the book, *The Golden Dawn,* Israel Regardie says:

"Thou shalt know that the whole Sphere of Sensation which surroundeth the whole physical body of a man is called 'The Magical Mirror of the Universe'. For therein are represented all the occult forces of the Universe projected as on a sphere, convex to the outer, but concave to man. This sphere surroundeth the physical body of man as the Celestial Heavens do the body of a Star or a Planet, having their forces mirrored in its atmosphere."

The magicians in The Golden Dawn believed that the Sphere of Sensation was an exact microcosm of the macrocosm of Universal Energies. They took the idea that God created humans in his own image. If the Universe in totality, both physically and spiritually, is God, then humans must have the energies of the Universe itself but in miniature form. They believed this was how the magician was able to perform works of magick and create change in the Universe in accordance to their personal will. Each and every human, once trained magically, has the ability to summon astrological, planetary, and spiritual energies and shape it towards their desire. This is because their Sphere of Sensation contains the totality of the Greater Universe just as a tiny piece of DNA genetically contains the totality of the human body.

I have practiced hermetic magick for over 20 years and I have come to understand that every human does indeed have a Sphere of Sensation just as every human being has an energetic aura. There are many things the hermetic magician can do with the Sphere of Sensation but for our purposes in this book I will limit this discussion to how you can use this magical technique in our psychic and psychopomp work.

The Sphere of Sensation can greatly help us develop our psychic abilities. One of the ways it can help us is that it can give us a model of how our consciousness is able to expand, contract, and interact with energies that are outside of our bodies and help us develop our perceptions of these energies. You must be thinking right now, "What is Chris talking about?" Let me clarify. Stop for a moment and think about what your consciousness is and how does it relate to outside stimulus. We are accustomed to how our consciousness interacts with outside stimulus with our five physical senses. Our eyes help us see outside stimulus, our ears help us hear outside stimulus, and so forth. But how does our consciousness interact with outside spiritual energies? This can be challenging to think about. Try this quick exercise:

Sphere of Sensation Exercise 1

1. Clear your mind of all distractions. Take a few deep breaths and place yourself in a light trance.
2. Imagine you have a sphere of energy (I see it as clear or translucent) around your body that takes up about the same space as your aura. This is your Sphere of Sensation or your outside consciousness.
3. Close your eyes and imagine your Sphere of Sensation expanding to take up the entire room.
4. Without opening your eyes, allow your Sphere of Sensation to become aware of every single thing in the room.
5. What things did you become aware of? How did you feel while you were performing this technique?
6. When you are ready, bring your Sphere of Sensation back to the size of your aura.
7. Journal your experience.

Normally, the Sphere of Sensation helps you become very aware of every single thing in the room. How you experience this feeling is unique to you , but for me it feels kind of like my nerves are able to feel objects that my body is not touching. If you do not have the same experience as me that is ok. What is your experience?

Sphere of Sensation Exercise 2

1. Take a walk outside. It can be in the city or countryside.
2. Clear your mind of all distractions. Take a few deep breaths and place yourself in a light trance.
3. Imagine you have a sphere of energy (I see it as clear or translucent) around your body that takes up about the same space as your aura. This is your Sphere of Sensation or your outside consciousness.
4. Imagine your Sphere of Sensation expands to encompass about one block.
5. Become aware of everything within your expanded sphere. Become aware of the people, animals, trees, birds, homes, buildings, and anything else that your Sphere of Sensation encompasses.
6. Take note of the impressions you are receiving by each of these things. How do they feel to you? What do their energies feel like? What other information are you getting from each of these things?
7. When you are ready bring your Sphere of Sensation back to the size of your aura.
8. Journal your experience.

The Empathic Psychic

An Empath is someone who has the psychic ability to feel another person's emotions. They can feel exactly what someone else is feeling. Psychic empathy is perhaps one of the more common psychic abilities. Being an empath is not the same thing as being intuitive. Many beginners have come to believe that when their intuitive abilities are becoming stronger that they are an empath. This is not what being an empath means. When you are able connect to someone's emotions and feel what the other person is feeling, that is being an empath. Being an empath has many benefits when working with the spirits of the dead. In order to effectively help a spirit transition to the

Land of the Ancestors, we must listen to their story and do our best to understand why they are unable to transition into the spirit world. Sometimes, the spirit is confused, angry, or heart broken, and they are having a hard time telling their story or explaining to you how they are feeling. When we can feel their emotions through empathy, we can better understand what they are going through.

For many psychics and witches, the power of empathy is one of the first psychic techniques that they develop. Some people are able to develop this skill naturally, while other have to practice at it. Either way, this ability must be practiced in order to be fully effective in psychopomp work. When I was practicing my psychic skills years ago, my empathic ability grew at an exceptional pace. I felt everything. And I mean everything! I had a hard time walking down the street without feeling the emotions of every single person in a two-block radius. Some of their emotions were so heavy, I was not sure if I wanted to cry or to just run away. Going into a crowded room or bar was painful. All the emotions would hit me all at the same time. I do not tell you this to boast of my empathy skills, but rather to give you a warning. You must center, ground, and shield yourself so that you are not overwhelmed by the rushing emotions. When I am doing psychic work and I need to dampen the amount of emotions from someone I am feeling, I will shield myself and program my energy shield to only allow enough of the emotional energy to come through so that I can get an accurate reading on them. This will help your empathic energies become more refined and you will find you are better able to use your gift.

I have come to think that empathy is one of the more difficult psychic skills to understand and use effectively. Some people are naturally more emotional than others. Some people have the ability to control their emotions more than others do. We all have had those days that we are depressed, happy, sad, or angry and not really sure why. There are a myriad of reasons why we may feel a particular way on a particular day. However, when we are picking up someone else's emotions we may mistakenly think that the emotions we are feeling are our own. I have had several occasions where my emotions became jumbled up with another person's emotions and it was hard to distinguish whose emotion was whose. There are a few questions I will ask myself to help distinguish my own emotions from someone else's emotions.

1. Did something happen to prompt this particular emotion?
2. Is there an emotion I could be repressing that is working its way out?
3. Am I over tired, hungry, or excited about something?
4. Does this feel like my emotion or could I be picking it up from someone else?
5. Have I energetically cleaned my body from emotional attachments sent to me unintentionally?

After asking yourself these questions and determining the emotions you are experiencing are not yours, it may be beneficial to figure out where the emotions are coming from. I do this by tuning in to each person in the room. My senses will become stronger when I get to the right person.

Using your powers of empathy is very helpful in your psychopomp work. In order to help the spirit of the dead cross over to the Land of the Ancestors it is important to understand why they were not able to leave the earthly plane. I have come across many spirits who were not able to articulate their story very well, but I was able to connect to their emotions and really understand how they were feeling. This gave me better insight on how to effectively convince them to leave their earthly life behind and travel back home with their ancestors. Your empathic powers will also be extremely valuable when you learn to read the psychic energies in someone's home after they call for your help with a haunting.

In order to control and strengthen your empathic abilities, perform these two empath exercises.

Empath Exercise 1

For this exercise you will need a partner to help you. Both of you sit in a chair facing each other. Ask your partner to relax as much as they can and simply enjoy the experience.

1. Take a moment and take stock of your own emotions. How are you feeling? What are your emotions at this very moment? Are there any emotions that are deep in your heart that you should be aware of?
2. Clear your mind and take a few deep breaths and relax your body as much as you can.
3. Imagine your heart chakra opening up like a flower. Now, imagine that your powers of empathy reside in your heart chakra as a small sphere of light.
4. Visualize the empathic sphere growing larger and larger until it encompasses both yourself and the other person.
5. Without judgement, what emotions are you feeling from the other person? How does sensing someone else's emotions make you feel? What information are you getting by these emotions?
6. Disengage from the other person's emotions. Visualize your empathic sphere becoming smaller and smaller until it sits back into your heart chakra.
7. Center, ground, shield, and journal your experience.

Empath Exercise 2

For this exercise you can ask a friend to help you or you can simply go out into the "field" and practice this work. If you are doing this exercise in the field, make sure that you are not in an overcrowded place. If you are new to this type of work, crowds can sometimes send too much emotional energy that can be overwhelming at first. Always remember to center, shield, and ground with this type of work.

1. Take a moment and take stock of your own emotions. How are you feeling? What are your emotions at this very moment? Are there any emotions that are deep in your heart that you should be aware of?
2. Clear your mind and take a few deep breaths and relax your body as much as you can.
3. Visualize your heart chakra opening up like a flower. Focus on your power of empathy that resides in your heart as a sphere.
4. Choose someone that you would like to sense their emotions. It can be any person you like.
5. See your empathic sphere expanding to the size of your heart chakra. Now, imagine that your heart chakra sends out a beam of empathic psychic energy to the person who you are sensing. Try to be as gentle as you can with this. Sensitive people will be able to tell you are "probing" them.
6. What emotions are you sensing from the other person? What information are you getting about this person from their emotions?
7. Gently disengage your empathic beam from the person.
8. Journal your experience.

Psychometry

Psychometry is the psychic art of touching a piece of jewelry, cloths, keys, or any personal item belonging to someone and being able to read the psychic impressions of the owner. The science behind this ability is that our own personal energy, or life force, has a unique vibration that is specific to each person. Some psychics and witches call this an energy signature. We leave our energy signature on every single thing we touch. In fact, our bodies emit our personal energy all the time leaving a trail of our energy in every room we enter and even walking down the street. Normally, this energy dissipates because we only leave behind a certain amount. Our personal belongings have a buildup of our personal energy and a psychic or a witch has the ability to use our energy signature as a link to us. Essentially, this is one of the reasons why we are able to take a personal object and use it as a link to our target in magical spells.

In our psychopomp work, psychometry is important because this skill can tell us more about the spirit we are working with. By touching the objects, the spirit was connected to, we will be able to reach into the past, present, and future of the spirit through our mind. There have been many times when someone has come to me asking me to help their loved one cross over. Before I agree to do any type of spirit work, I always assess the situation. I need to find out what is actually happening in a person's home. There have been cases where someone was being haunted and they just knew it was their grandfather when in actuality it was a different spirit, or it was simply their imagination. Using psychometry can give you a better view of the whole story. By touching a personal object once belonging to the spirit you will be able to tune into the energy signature of the deceased. This will help you find the spirit in the spirit world.

Psychometry Exercise 1

For this exercise you will need a friend's personal belonging such as jewelry, keys, glasses, or anything else that has their energy.

1. Take a few deep breaths and clear your mind and relax your body the best you can. Take a few more deep breaths and allow yourself to go into a light trance state.

2. Hold the personal item in your non-dominant hand.

3. Allow your energies to open up and become receptive to the energies of the personal item. You can try one of these techniques:

    A. Simply hold the personal item in your hand and wait for impressions to appear in your mind.

    B. Open your Sphere of Sensation and expand it to encompass the personal item in your hand.

    C. Imagine your hand has its own Sphere of Sensation. Expand the hands sphere of sensation to encompass the personal item.

    D. Place your consciousness into the center of the personal item. You can do this by visualizing your consciousness as a share of white light in your mind. Visualize this sphere of your consciousness traveling from your mind to the center of the personal item.

4. What are you perceiving from your psychometry reading? You may only feel a vibration, heat or cold, or you may see colors and symbols. All of these things give you clues to the energies.

5. Practice your preferred technique daily. After a while, you will be able to see images and eventually whole scenes and scenarios.

6. Journal your experience.

Psychometry Exercise 2

1. Take a few deep breaths and clear your mind and relax your body the best you can. Take a few more deep breaths and allow yourself to go into a light trance state.

2. Hold the personal item in both of your hands. Take a

moment to tune in to the energies of the personal item.

3. Ask questions like, "Tell me about this person's past", "How can I communicate in a way this person will understand?", or "Show me what happened to this person."

4. Imagine your Sphere of Sensation expanding to encompass the personal item in your hands. Now, visualize your brow chakra expanding to also encompass the personal item. Alternately, you can send a beam of energy from your brow chakra to the personal item after you have expanded your Sphere of Sensation.

5. Ask your question softly to yourself and know with all of your being that the energies will show you the answers that you seek. Try not to judge the images you see. You may see a scenario as though you are watching a movie. Or you may see symbols or hear voices in your mind. Allow the information to come through as it will.

6. When you are ready, disengage your brow chakra and bring it back to its normal size. Next, bring your Sphere of Sensation back to its normal size.

7. Journal your experience.

Pendulum

The pendulum is a magical tool that can be used when you are learning to communicate with the spirits. The spirits of the dead can move the pendulum in such a way to communicate with the living. Traditionally, this tool is made from a crystal, stone, ring, or coin that is suspended by a chord. The chord can be made from a string, ribbon, yarn, chain, or necklace. The one I have is a quartz crystal that hangs from a silver chain. Clear quartz is one of my favorite crystals and I like how it feels energetically. You can choose any type of stone or crystal that feels good to you. A ring or small weight tied to a string will work in a pinch. There is really no right or wrong way that a pendulum has to be made. It all depends on what you like.

There are several books on the market about how to use a pendulum, but it is perhaps one of the easiest tools to use when it comes to spirit communication. The pendulum is used in a similar way as a Ouija Board in that the practitioner physically touches the tool in order for the spirit to connect it to their life force to manifest the physical movement of the weight. The movement of the weight is moved to signal "Yes" or "No" answers. Advanced practitioners can use the pendulum to spell out words, phrases, and sometimes sentences. I have found that is more effective to ask the spirits yes or no questions. When you ask a spirit to spell out words, the energies can sometimes become jumbled and the words can be misspelled or confused leading the spirit to feel frustrated. Oftentimes, when a spirit we are speaking with begins to feel frustrated, they will leave the room or disconnect energetically from you which may quickly end your spirit session. There are many ways to hold the pendulum. I prefer to hold the chain in my dominate hand and dangle the weighted portion over my non-dominate hand, palm-up. This will create an energetic circuit that the spirit can tap into so that they can move the pendulum.

Speaking to Spirits with the Pendulum

1. Take a few deep breaths and clear your mind and relax your body. Place yourself in a light trance.
2. Hold the pendulum chord with your dominant hand over your non-dominant hand, palm facing up. For right-handed people, hold the chord with your right hand over your left palm. For left-handed people, hold the chord with your left hand over your right palm.
3. Open your heart charka to the energies in the room. Try to feel the energies as best as you can.
4. Expand your Sphere of Sensation to encompass the room. I mentally program my Sphere of Sensation to

allow spirits of the dead to come through the pendulum.

5. Try to connect with the spirit the best you can. If you are not sure who the spirit is you can say to yourself, **"I wish to speak with any spirit of the dead who is here now."**

6. Once you feel you are connected to the energies in the room, ask the spirit (through the pendulum) to show you "yes". The pendulum will move in one direction. Then ask the spirit to show you "no". The pendulum will then move in a different direction.

7. Ask yes or no questions. You can ask things like "Do you need my help?" or "Do you have unfinished business here?" You can ask any question you like, but make sure it is worded so that the spirit can answer yes or no.

8. When you are ready, tell the spirit goodbye and disconnect from the spirit. Retract your Sphere of Sensation back to your aura.

9. Journal your experience.

Scrying

Scrying is the ancient art of peering into the astral universe by the power of the psychic mind. It is usually performed with some kind of medium in order to receive messages from the unseen world. There are many devices that can be used to aid you in scrying such as bowls, crystals, magick mirrors, and many other items. The art of scrying has been done for thousands of years. We know the Egyptians used the oil from lamps in order to see into the otherworlds. Nostradamus, the famous prophet, used the method of water scrying in order to see his visions of the future. Dr. John Dee, the personal astrologer to Queen Elizabeth I, and his partner Edward Kelly, used the obsidian mirror to speak with angels in order to learn Enochian Angelic Magick. Take a moment to imagine the witch or Spirit Walker gazing into a still pond that reflects the starry night sky. This starry pond would be the perfect scrying device to speak with the spirits.

How scrying works is that when you gaze upon your scrying device, such as a black bowl, the chatter in the everyday conscious mind will step aside so that the psychic power of your subconscious mind can come through. As you know, it is the subconscious that is able to perceive subtle energies and astral forms, not your physical eyes. The subconscious then must take these energies and give them a form of some kind in order for them to make sense to the conscious mind. In the beginning of your practice, you may see colors, flashes of light, or pictures that seem formless. This is ok because your mind is not used to seeing energies like this, so it is doing the best it can. After regular practice, the forms will become clearer and easier for you to understand. Think of it like learning to exercise for the first time. At first you will feel uncoordinated and wobbly, but after a few weeks you will be able to do the exercise with a lot more ease and success.

Scrying is one of the best ways for the student to begin to learn to work with the energies of the spirits of the dead. Until you are able to see the spirits on the physical plane, using a scrying device can be greatly beneficial with your psychopomp work practice. When using a scrying device, keep in mind it is only a tool to focus your mind and strengthen your psychic ability of perceiving the spirits. The magick is not coming from the tool. The magick is coming from you. The scrying tool is only helping your mind to focus.

When you are first learning how to scry, I would suggest you begin with either a black bowl filled with fresh water or a black magick mirror. If you use a black bowl, any bowl will do. Mine is a ceramic black bowl that I bought for 99 cents at a street vendor in New York City when I used to live there. You can fill your bowl with fresh water or from a natural source such as a lake, pond, or river but filtered water will do as wellIf you would like to use a magick mirror, you can make your own or find one at a metaphysical store. I find that it is better to practice at night in a dark room. The only illumination should come from a single candle flame that is placed far enough away from your bowl or mirror that you cannot see the flame reflected in the device. I have found that having incense conducive to psychic work helps me tremendously. Any incense that makes you feel magical will do, but some that are known to enhance psychic powers are sage, mugwort, wormwood, rose, and copal. I have also found it helpful to call upon your Psychopomp Teacher when you practice scrying. When you call them, ask them to help you strengthen your psychic abilities in order to work with the spirits in a more tangible way.

One of the magical secrets to help you to see the spirits of the dead in the scrying bowl or mirror is to energetically connect the device to the waters of the Underworld. Remember, the sacred waters of the Underworld have the ability to reveal the past, present, and future, as well as being a conduit for the spirits to manifest. They can pull the energies of the waters in order to come reveal themselves to us in magick.

To Scry with the Spirits of the Dead

Items needed:
Black bowl with water or magick mirror
Incense
Single Candle

1. Place your mirror or bowl in front of you and turn off the lights. Light your single candle and your incense.
2. Take a few deep breaths and place yourself in a light trance state.
3. Open your heart and brow chakra.
4. Call to your Psychopomp Teacher and ask them to aid you in your scrying magick tonight.
5. If you like, you can say prayers to your gods or goddesses

to help you in your scrying work.

6. Place your hands over your bowl or mirror. Visualize the magical waters of the Underworld. See them flowing from the Underworld to your bowl or mirror. Spend some time with this. Know with all of your being that you are no longer gazing into a bowl or mirror; you are gazing straight into the waters of the Underworld.

7. Take a deep breath and breathe your magick into the bowl or mirror. The energies of the Underworld blend with your energies of life and magick.

8. Now, look deep into the bowl or mirror. Look beyond the surface. Pretend that you are looking 10 feet below the surface as if you were looking 10 feet into a swimming pool or lake.

9. Call to the spirit you wish to see or simply state that you wish to communicate to a spirit who wishes to communicate with you.

10. Take all the time you need to see the energies. You may see colors, flashing lights, fog, or mists. This is good. It means you mind is perceiving the energies.

11. Once you see the spirit or what you feel is the spirit you may ask simple questions such as: their name, where they lived in life, and what they did for a living. If you cannot hear them, try to feel the answers. Tap into your intuition the best you can.

12. When you are ready, say your goodbyes to the spirit and to your Psychopomp Teacher and end the session.

If you did not perceive anything from this scrying session that is perfectly fine. Many people do not see or hear anything their first few times. The trick is to keep practicing this technique each day until your psychic abilities become stronger and stronger.

Chapter 5

Helping the Dying to Transition

"The dying are our teachers, and each generation's parting gift is showing us how to go about the journey of dying. They are just a few steps ahead of us in the great scheme of cosmic time, and they are marking the way for when it is our turn."
-Felicity Warner, *The Soul Midwives Handbook: The Holistic And Spiritual Care of the Dying*

The End of Life

Each person experiences the end of life in their own unique way. We are all individuals and have a different way that we choose to live and go through our lives. This is also how we approach death. A life that is loving and well lived will most likely experience the final days with a similar energy. Those whose lives are filled with bitterness and regret will most likely take this energy into their final days. Some will fear death. They may fear the pain and suffering they could experience while others fear the uncertainties that death brings. Then there are those who fear that death is a final end of consciousness and everything they worked to become will be lost. Some will embrace death. They have a strong spiritual faith that speaks to them and gives them purpose. There are also those who have lived through so many experiences in life that they are ready to step into death with an open heart. No two people will have the exact same feelings towards death. These feelings and thoughts are as unique as they are.

Many people in our modern culture have not taken the time to think about their feelings about death. Often times, instead of embracing our inevitable fate of dying, we push it out of our minds so that we are not confronted with our own fears of mortality. Death is something that happens to other people, never to us or our loved ones. We have even become desensitized to many aspects of death. The nightly news consistently has reports of murders, gang violence, and car accidents. We even see movies that depicts violence and death on a regular basis. With things like this, death may not seem real to us. It is something that happens to other people, but not to us. When someone is approaching death, this is the time to contemplate and come to an understanding of their own death. Some people will gracefully begin this process at the end of life, while others will not. Just as we cannot force someone to spiritually evolve, we cannot force someone to accept their own death. This is a spiritual journey that is all their own. We can support the dying the best we can, but their path is for them to walk.

How to Support the Dying

There are many ways that we can support the dying. When we are helping a person transition into death on an energetic and spiritual level this is psychopomp work. We are guiding their spirit from the physical plane to the spiritual plane. When we are helping the dying emotionally, physically, and somewhat spiritually, this is commonly referred to Death Midwife or Death Doula. In her book *The Art of Death Midwifery: An Introduction and Beginner's Guide,* Joellyn St. Pierre, D.Div. says:

"The art of death midwifery is a profound and intuitive way of communing with the dying, of lending support and guidance to those making the greatest of transitions. Committing to deep spiritual work. The death midwife becomes a strong, clear, conduit who directs the flow of divine love to the dying."

There are many ways that a Death Midwife is able to help a person transition into death. They are able to help on a very practical level by helping them plan for their funeral and asking important questions about the process that they may not know to ask. They can also help the person plan a home funeral if that is something they choose to do. They can also assist them in making sure they have all the required legal documents completed as well as to decide what to do with the remains once the person has transitioned.

The Death Midwife is there for the dying. The family may be grieving and coming to terms with the death of their loved one, but you are there for the person who is transitioning. There are times when the Death Midwife will hold silent vigil for the person. Holding a vigil is a sacred act of being present and holding space. It may seem like you are not doing something sacred, but simply being there if they need you or bearing witness to this sacred spiritual process is magical in itself. In the U.S., we tend to put a lot of emphasis on "doing something" rather than supporting the process that is already happening. I will admit that I am a "fixer". It is in my nature to help and make it better. I will find myself troubleshooting ideas until I find a feasible solution to whatever problem I am faced with at the time. In Death Midwife work, we are not trying to help or "fix" a person. We are aiding their natural transition into death. Holding a vigil is an act of being present during someone's sacred process of death. We are a witness to this beautiful process from the physical plane to a place of spirit.

Another thing we can do to make the dying more comfortable is to do gentle therapeutic touch. I have been a licensed massage therapist for many years, and I have learned that human touch has a powerful healing effect. Not just on the physical body, but on the emotions and general wellbeing of the person as well. Therapeutic touch can be as simple as holding someone's hand or placing your hand on their leg or knee if that is appropriate. With permission, you can stroke their hair or gently massage their scalp. Therapeutic touch establishes an energetic connection between you and the dying. You do not have to do anything special or massage them per se, by touching them you are showing support and letting them know that you are there for them. People tend to be afraid to touch the dying. They can be afraid that they can harm them in some way if they reach out to them. If you remember to avoid any ports, tubes, injection sites, wounds, or anything you are unfamiliar with you should be ok. Again, holding the hand is wonderful in itself. We can also play music that feels special and perhaps even spiritual to them. Music is powerful and can transport us to many places. Music fills our world with magick and wonder. Music can help make the dying person more comfortable and can help their emotional wellbeing.

By being present with the dying person we have the opportunity to encourage them to tell us stories about their life. All lives are sacred and have spiritual meaning. Not everyone will be mentioned in history books or in newspapers. Even still, everyone's life and experiences are sacred. If you notice in this chapter, I use the word "experience" several times. This is intentional because life is a series of experiences that happen on many different levels. We have physical experiences, emotional experiences, energetic experiences, and mental experiences. All of these things are a part of the dying person's life. Each one of these things made the person who they are. If the person is willing, we can ask them to share some of their experiences that they had. If possible, it is also a good idea to ask them to write down their experiences for their family members and perhaps the next generation of their family. They may think their life is nothing special and ordinary, but to the next generation, our experiences in this time right now will seem magical to them. It will also help the family understand the person just a little bit better than they did. Never underestimate the power of telling the story of one's life.

Emotional support to the dying person is an act of healing

in itself. When we are attending a dying person, our role may not be that of pastoral counselor or therapist, but we can still be present for their emotional needs. We can imagine how we might feel if we found out that we were dying. We can close our eyes and pretend to hear news that we only have a short time to live. We can imagine what we might feel like in these scenarios, but we will never know what the person's emotions truly are. Even if we have the exact same circumstances as the dying person, everyone's emotions are unique to themselves. We can be supportive of the person's emotions by listening to what they have to say and being present with them without having judgement or seeking to fix their emotions. The act of listening is very powerful. There may be things that the dying wish to express to someone before they die. Oftentimes, the dying will confide in a person they do not know very well before they would confide in a family member. Families can have complicated feelings especially when it comes to the person transitioning. The dying may not wish to complicate things further so they may express themselves to a caregiver, healer, or minister. You may experience that some days the person will want to talk and some days they will not. It is not up to us to judge what is good for them, but to support them by being present to what they need at the time. During the final days and hours, the person may be too weak or incoherent and talking may be sporadic. At this time, we can still support them emotionally by being present for them holding vigil.

If you are a member of the person's clergy, my advice to you is to be there in the role that they need. If they are looking for spiritual answers and advice, by all means, be there for them in that capacity and give them the spiritual support that they may need. However, as ministers, we can still be supportive by simply being present for them.

Energy Healing Techniques

As witches, Spirit Walkers, and energy healers, we have the unique ability to send healing energy to the dying. The word "healing" does not always mean to regenerate wounded cells and tissues and vitalize the body for perfect health. The meaning of *healing* is to bring someone back into the best possible balance that they are able in regard to the circumstances that they are in. As much as someone may want to be a hero and "save" everyone and help them live longer, that is not the role of the healer. Healers bring more than the physical regeneration of the body. Healers also bring energies to someone in order to balance their energy bodies in such a way that they can better understand and cope with the circumstances they are in. When we simplify the term *healing,* it means to balance.

We can do a lot of good by sending healing energy to the dying. We can make them more comfortable physically. They may be in some pain that we can help alleviate with energy healing. If they are in the hospital or hospice the doctors can give them medication to control the pain. This can make the person feel confused and very groggy, and some people may opt out of this. Some spiritual practices, such as Buddhism, may warn that too much pain medication may make the person too groggy to concentrate on the journey of death during transition. Energy healing cannot alleviate all of someone's pain, but it will dampen it so that they are comfortable.

Energy healing can aid the dying by helping to balance their emotions. There are so many emotions that the dying may experience, it can be overwhelming to them. During the five stages of grief there is denial, anger, bargaining, depression, and acceptance. They may experience one or more of these emotions. There is not a right or wrong way to grieve one's own death, and we must honor the emotions they are feeling. But we can bring balancing energy to them, so they are not overwhelmed with emotion. One of the beautiful things about energy healing is that we are not forcing healing or balance upon someone. They can take the energy or not, according to their will. It is always a good idea to get their permission before we do any energy healing, especially emotional healing and balancing. They may need to experience their emotions as they come. However, some may ask that you send energy healing so they can process the emotions in a way that is better for them.

Energy healing can help the dying balance the energies that are flowing in their body. As we know, chakras are the major energy centers along the spine that help regulate energy from the earth and heavens for proper function of the physical and energy bodies. When a person begins to die and transition into death, their chakras will begin to unravel. This will allow the energy bodies to disengage from the physical body. Again, by sending healing energy, we are not seeking to fix someone or to make them physically better. We are sending healing energy to help the chakras and meridians prepare for death. The healing energies will give the chakras and meridians the balancing power that they need to begin disengaging from the body and release the spirit. This is helpful because it will aid the disengagement process of the chakras for a smoother and more comfortable transition into death.

Energy healing for the dying, I find, is very helpful. I have been doing energy healing for a very long time, and I am very confident in it. That being said, there is no rule that says you have to do energy healing on someone who is transitioning. My rule of thumb is, when in doubt, check in with your gods, guides, and Psychopomp Teacher. If it does not feel right to do energy healing, then do not do it. Perhaps the dying person's spirits and guides have something already planned out that will benefit their spiritual process. Normally, energy healing cannot hurt anything; because, if it is not meant for the person, then it will not have any effect or the person's spirits will void the energy. Always use your judgment and listen to your instincts.

A big part of energy healing is calling upon your healing gods, guides, and ancestors. Just as there is a team of doctors who perform surgeries on a patient so, too, do we have a spiritual team that helps us perform energy work. This is one of the reasons why it is so important to have gods, ancestors, guides, and a Psychopomp Teacher that helps you with the process of death and dying. They will help perform the best energy healing that is better suited to the dying person. In my healing practice, my healing spirits and gods help me a great deal. Just when I have a treatment plan for my client, they often advise me to alter it or change my healing session in some way. They will show me a magical symbol or picture that I should place in a person's energy body or chakra that will greatly benefit the healing of that person. As I have said many times before, the gods and spirits can see energies that we cannot. They have a better understanding of the energetic ebb and flow of what is happening with the person we are doing the healing treatment with. When it comes to the dying, the gods and spirits have a deep level of understanding and compassion. Before you do any energy healing for the dying, make sure that you pray to your spirits and gods and ask them to help you in your treatment. When the spirits appear, tune into their energies. Allow their energies to join with yours. Feel the energies between yourself and the spirits synchronize and join together. When you connect with the spirits in this way, not only are you strengthening your powers of healing, but you are performing the energy healing with the union of mind and spirit for the highest good of the dying.

Sending Healing Energy

When you are using energy healing for a person who is transitioning, you can use Reiki if you are trained in that modality. If you are not attuned to Reiki or another form of energy healing, that is ok. You can use general energy healing techniques from the Universe. Any energy technique that uses celestial energy will be beneficial to the person. However, I will caution against energy techniques that utilizes energies from the Earth Mother. Earth energies tend to be very grounding and may inhibit the dying person from leaving their physical body smoothly. Modalities such as Quantum Healing use earth energies and are very grounding for the body.

For this energy technique, we will be using general healing energy from the celestial realm. You do not have to be specifically trained in energy work to perform this technique effectively.

1. Close your eyes and take a few deep cleansing breaths. Center yourself in this space and open your crown and heart chakras.
2. Pray to your gods, spirits, and Psychopomp Teacher for guidance through this healing process.
3. Bring your consciousness to the vast reaches of the Universe in the Upperworld. Know that the building blocks of creation, harmony, and balance are implicit in the energies of the heavens.
4. Bring your attention to your heart chakra. Have the intent to send balancing energies to the person. Have a deep knowledge that whatever energies they need for balance will come through you today.
5. Ask if you may place your hands on the person. If that is not appropriate, you may hover over them. You do not need to be close to the person. You can direct the flow of energy from anywhere in the room.
6. Bring your conscious awareness to the center of the Universe. Take a deep breath, and on the inhale, visualize the healing energy coming from the Universe and then pouring down into your crown chakra and then into to your heart chakra. I see it as white light, but whatever color comes through to you will be the color you need

that day. Trust that your guides and your intuition know what is best.

7. Take another deep breath and on the exhale. Visualize the healing energy moving from your heart chakra, through your arms, and out of your hands to the person to whom you are sending the energy. Visualize this energy as a continual stream of healing energy.

8. Spend as much time as you need. If you like, you may ask your gods, guides, and Psychopomp Teacher to help you with this process. I will sometimes see them sending healing energy as well.

9. When you are ready to conclude, stop the visualization. This will stop the energy flow and cut the energy cord between you and the other person. Thank your spirits and guides for their help and thank the Universe for sending the energies though you.

The Energies of Support

We all need someone to support us from time to time. As human beings we need each other. We need someone in our times of joy. When we have a job promotion, starting a new relationship, or celebrating a birth, we need people to share in our happiness. I cannot tell you how many times I was so excited about something and I said, "I just needed to share this exciting news with someone!" We also need someone in our times of sorrow. When an important relationship ends, we lose a job, or when we are sick, we need someone to help us through the dark and troubled times. In our grief, we also need someone from time to time. Everyone grieves differently, but at times we may need someone to be with us even if we realize it or not. When someone is in the process of dying, they need us. The closer they come to the time of death, the more they will need support. During the process of dying, the person may not be able to articulate what they need. They may even be unconscious, but they still need our support.

There will come a time in the death process when the healing energy is doing all it can, and we will have to give them the energy of support at these last moments until death comes upon them. There is more energy work that needs to be done, but instead of the energies of healing and balance, now are the energies of love and support. As we are well aware, the person may have fears, regrets, and other concerns about their own journey into death. They need the energies of love and support the most now. You are a healer. Healing comes from the love and compassion we have for all beings upon the Earth. Now is the time to send the energies of love to the dying.

1. In quietness and stillness, center, ground, and shield yourself. You may have unexpected emotions that come up and doing this basic energy work for ourselves will keep us focused on the person who needs us.

2. Open your heart chakra. Close your eyes and tune in to the love of the Universe. All of creation in the Universe is made of love. It is Universal love that created all things and it is Universal love that transitions us into death. Know that love permeates every aspect of the Universe.

3. Take a breath and inhale the Universal love into our heart chakra and into our whole body. Feel the love energies flowing through you.

4. Take another breath and on the exhale send Universal love to the dying person. You can send the energy through your hands or directly through your heart chakra. Visualize them being cocooned in this warm, gentle, soothing Universal love.

5. You can connect to their mind and tell them telepathically, "You are safe. You are loved. You are supported."

6. Spend as much time as you like with this process.

7. When you are ready, stop the flow of energy and

cut the energy chord. Thank your gods, guides, and Psychopomp Teacher.

If you cannot be in the same room with the dying person, do this energy work while spirit journeying or distance healing.

The Process of Dying

When the sacred time comes when a person is actively dying, there is an energetic process that takes place in order for the spirit to be released from the physical body. As we know, the physical body is supported by the chakras and the elements that they represent. Each chakra has an important function that keeps the body healthy and working to the best of its ability. The major chakras that reside along the spine keep the body and its organs healthy. One of the main tasks that the chakras have, is to take the life force energies from the earth and the Universe and to convert them into usable energy so that the body and its organs can function in a healthy way. The chakras govern the part of the body that they are closest to. For example, the crown chakra governs the brain; the brow governs the eyes, ears, and mouth; the throat chakra governs the throat; and the heart chakra governs the heart and lungs, and so forth. Without healthy chakras, the body would not be able to process the energies needed to energetically nourish the body.

When the body is actively dying, the energies of the chakras are disrupted and begin to unravel. As the chakras are unraveling, the elements begin to leave the body as well. This allows the energies of the body to subside and return back to the Universe. Once the chakras are disengaged and return to the energy worlds, the physical body will no longer function. With the physical body no longer connected to the astral and spiritual bodies through the chakras, it is able to be discarded by the subtler energy bodies and the spirit is able to cross over into the realm of the ancestors.

Earth Dissolves into Water

When we are in the womb of our mother, we are connected to her by the umbilical cord. We are given nourishment and life sustaining elements through the chord that is attached near our navel chakra. Our navel chakra is associated with the element of water. This is because this is the part of the body that has many fluids that aid in food digestion. An interesting thing to note is that our colon helps regulate heat in our body. As the navel chakra gave us life at the beginning of our incarnation upon Earth, it is the chakra that begins our death process so that we can take our journey into the world of spirit. During this process, the dying person's body will begin to feel heavy and may have a sinking feeling. They may not be able to move much on their own. Because the water element in the navel chakra regulates our body heat, the person may begin to feel very warm or overheated. Their cognitive functions will begin to slow. They may start to process information more slowly. They may also begin staring off into space and experiencing what doctors call "hallucinations". It is common for the dying to see their ancestors and friends who have died many years before. As the body begins to go closer to death, their awareness will also begin to go closer to the spirit world.

Water Dissolves into Fire

We are emotional creatures. We are able to feel love and compassion through our heart chakra. When we have a difficult decision to make, people will often tell us to "listen to our heart". The heart chakra is also the place where healing energy from the Universe is sent before it goes through our arms and hands. In order to give effective energy healing the heart chakra must infuse the energy with compassion and love. With the dissolution of the watery navel chakra into the fiery solar plexus, the heart chakra can no longer be sustained, and it too begins to unravel. The element of fire is now dominant in the body and the dying person may have a dry mouth and the kidneys will shut down. The pervasive fire energy may cause the person to become agitated or perhaps frightened of what is happening. Their mind may start to become erratic and they can go back and forth between clarity and fogginess of thought. They may also begin to perceive the energies of the spirit world more clearly.

Fire Dissolves into Air

Each of us has a special voice. It is through our voice that we can share our truth. Our truth is individual. Our truth may not be "true" for someone else, but it is true for us. It is an expression of who we are. When people are feeling the injustice of society it is their voice that inspires people to rise up and take a stand. It is a call to empowerment of the self as well as inspiring others to feel empowered as well. When the throat chakra dissolves the heat from the body begins to dissolve as well. The dying person may begin to feel cold and need more warmth. Having an extra blanket nearby will be very helpful. As the immune system dissolves and the liver shut downs, the vision becomes more blurred and out of focus and the mind continues to deteriorate.

Air Dissolves into Consciousness

Our consciousness is our everyday awareness. It is how we perceive the world. It is also how we dream. It is with our brow chakra that we dream ourselves into the spirit worlds and commune with the beings who reside there. Humans tend to associate the idea of our consciousness to our chatter or inner monologue that we have with ourselves every day. Our consciousness is so much more than this. It also contains our memories, our hopes and desires, our regrets, and even our fears. It is who we are upon this Earth and in the land of dreams. When our brow chakra dissolves, our root chakra is also dissolved. The dying person may begin to shake and lose control over their body. Their breathing begins to slow, and their eyes may roll back. Their emotions begin to calm and they may start to see memories of their life. If the person was spiritual or had a particular faith, then it is at this time they see their deities and ancestors come through more strongly. The gods, spirits, and ancestors do not allow the person to die alone, and they are with them during the process. It is here they are perceived more clearly.

Consciousness Dissolves into Spirit

The energies have now left the body and the dying person has no physical perception of the physical world. The final chakra of the crown has unraveled and their astral body and spirit body are now disconnected from the physical body. The person is now in spirit and they are free to go with their gods and ancestors. With this, they have completed their journey on the physical plane and begin a new journey in the Land of the Ancestors.

Consciousness

Our consciousness has a lot of control over our energy bodies and our spirit. When we journey or astral project, we must make the conscious effort to disconnect from our physical body so that we may travel to the other worlds. Our mind is not the same thing as our spirit, but our mind has control over our energy bodies. When our bodies transition into death, we are still very aware and conscious of our death experience. This is one of the reasons why some people may choose not to cross over to the Land of the Ancestors at the time of their death. Each of us still has control over our circumstances. Our mind is fully aware and functioning, even if the physical brain no longer has any function and is considered clinically dead.

As we have learned, there are many reasons why someone may not cross over to the ancestral lands. What all of these reasons have in common is, that they are attached to something on the physical plane. It can be a person, an idea, a belief, a circumstance, or to many other things that the person may be attached. Attachments are karmic energies that are formed in the chakras. Remember, chakras help disperse Universal and earth energies within the body. So, when we build up attachments to something, the buildup occurs in the main seven chakras that are located in the center of our bodies. Each of these energy attachments that we have, create an opportunity for us to learn a spiritual lesson that are sometimes called karmas. The energies of karma are meant to teach us to spiritually evolve and are never a punishment. When we build up attachments in our chakras, it is the Universe's way of giving us a chance to learn something so we can be better people spiritually. The downside to this, is that when a person dies, if their spirit does not exit their body through the crown chakra, it may leave through another chakra. Through this, attachments and earthly concerns can attach to the spirit as they leave the body. If this happens, the person is more likely to have strong reasons not to journey to the Land of the Ancestors and remain earthbound.

If we perform energy work during the death process, we can guide the spirit to leave the body through the crown chakra and it is far less likely that earthly concerns will attach to the spirit. This will allow the spirit of the person to leave all earthly concerns behind and travel to the Land of the Ancestors in a way that is balanced and serene. This energy work is fairly easy to perform.

The Eighth Chakra – The Soul Star

Anyone who has been practicing magick, witchcraft, or energy work knows about the seven chakras. What many people do not know is that you have many more chakras than just the seven. Most of the other chakras are small and are located throughout the body, most notably in the joints of the body. There are also chakras that are located outside of the physical body. The eighth chakra is a few inches above the crown chakra. Various healers have different names for the eighth chakra, but I have heard it commonly called The Soul Star Chakra. This chakra connects you with your Higher Self as well as the Universal intelligence. This is also the chakra that connects you with your chosen deity. My matron deity is Diana. If I wanted to meditate on her divine energy, I would visualize her in all of her glory and radiance in the eighth chakra. It is here that I would be able to receive her energies and wisdom.

When we are doing energy work for the dying, the eighth chakra is especially important. Focusing on the eighth chakra will help the dying person connect to their chosen deity or Universal energies. By connecting to these energies, this will allow them to better understand their connection to the Universe and its offerings. This will help them understand that their life, as well as their death, has meaning in all of creation.

Energy Work for the Time of Death

When doing energy work for a person who is actively dying, you will need to make sure that the person is as comfortable as they are able. In a hospital or hospice situation, do the best you can. They may be connected to machines or dependent on medicines. I will often send the energy of comfort, calmness, and relaxation during this time. I see this energy as a pink color, but you should use whatever color works for you. It will be helpful if you know the person's religion. You will use *their* gods and spirits if you are able. If they do not have a specific religion, or you are unaware of their faith, you can simply use God/Goddess, The Creator, or The Universe. When performing energy work for the actively dying, send energy only to the heart chakra for peace and balance. Once the last breath as been taken, focus the energy to the eighth chakra. A portal to the Land of the Ancestors may open up at any time during the ceremony. Our focus is the energy work for the dying person. If the person's ancestors come during the ceremony, they may assist with the energy work if they choose.

1. Call upon your gods, ancestors, guides, and Psychopomp Teacher. Pray to them and ask them to assist you in this healing process.

2. You do not have to touch the person to perform the energy work. You can hover your hands over the person. If this is not possible, you can visualize yourself performing the work in your mind. This is essentially astral energy work.

3. Send the energy of balance, calmness, wholeness, and love to the person's heart chakra. You are bringing them into this state in order for them to transition in a whole and balanced way.

4. The energies of attachment can appear to us as energy chords connected to the person. If you perceive any energy chords that are preventing the person from dying in a peaceful way, cut them in your mind so they no longer are causing the person any negative thoughts or emotions. It is time to let these things go in order to transition in a place of wholeness and balance.

5. If the person is conscious, you can instruct them at this time to focus on their deity in the Soul Star Chakra. They can pray to them or simply visualize. It is ok if the person is not conscious or aware of their surroundings. In this event, you will perform all the needed energy work.

6. Continue to send energy to the heart chakra until the last breath is taken. Be prepared that this may take minutes or hours. It is ok to take breaks. You do not have to send a constant stream of energy to the person dying.

7. Once the last breath has been taken, focus on the Soul Star chakra. This is the chakra that connects them to

their deity or the Universe in general. If they follow a particular god or goddess, see them dwelling in the Soul Star chakra. If they have no specific god or goddess, you can see a bright light that is The Universe or The Creator. Send energy to the Soul Star chakra and visualize it becoming bright and vibrant.

8. Continue to send bright healing light energy to the Soul Star. Visualize the divine being becoming brighter and brighter. Now, visualize the divine being (or the Universal light) sending loving and compassionate energy down to the person's heart chakra making the person's spirit balanced, whole, and blissful.

9. Visualize the person's spirit absorbing this loving divine energy in the heart chakra. It is here that the person is becoming one with the divine. Now, see the person's spirit as a bright orb of light ascending up the spine and out of the crown chakra. They will then reappear with their ancestors. They will be at peace and balanced as they journey to the Land of the Ancestors.

10. Cut the cord between you and the person. Thank all of your spirits and guides. Once you are back home, leave offerings for them.

Energy Work for After Death

There are times when we will be asked to help in someone's transition into death. Some of us belong to a greater pagan community and they will be aware of the sacred psychopomp work that we do. Even if you do not belong to a magical community, there will be times in your life that you will be asked to sit at someone's bedside to give them energy, love, and peace to ease their transition. Our world can be unpredictable, and things happen. Not everyone has the opportunity to die in a hospital or their own home surrounded by their loved ones. Sometimes death comes very quickly and unexpectedly. People die of heart attacks and other health conditions of which they were unaware. People also die by car accidents and many other incidents that were not predictable. I have been asked many times why we witches do not always know when someone is going to die by an accident. Even the most psychic and clairvoyant of us are not always meant to know when it is time for someone to transition. The Fates and the gods often have their own plans for someone and will block the energies that tell us of their upcoming death. As healers and magical people, we will always do our best. That is all that can be asked.

When someone dies suddenly, they deserve the same magical care as those who are aware of their death. They deserve the same love and support as we give those whose bedside we come to. Even if we are aware of someone in the process of dying, we cannot always be in the room with them. As much as we care for the dying, it is impossible for us to be with them at every moment and every second. As silly as this sounds, we have to eventually get up and go to the bathroom or get something to eat. The magick of death is on its own time frame and comes when it chooses.

When I learned to do energy healing for the dying, I was very grateful and honored to be taught this beautiful gift. However, I was saddened because I had known many people who had died, including my father, many years previously. Did they not deserve the same energy healing? My teachers taught me that energy healing knows no time nor space, so we have the ability to go back in time to send healing energy to those who have died in the past. I also learned that for this same reason, we can send energy healing to those who have died many miles away. I was overwhelmed with gratitude and joy to know that no matter when and no matter where someone died, we can still do energy work for them to help them transition into death with peace, love, and wholeness.

The energy work technique for someone who has died in

the past or from a long distance away is similar to that of when you are in the same room with someone. The difference is that, instead of being next to them, you are summoning their spirit in a loving and gentle way. To begin with, it is better to set up your space in a ritual setting. Light your candles and altar. Light some incense that feels magical and healing to you. Make sure you will be undisturbed for the duration of the ceremony.

Ceremony to Send Healing Energy to Someone who has Died

1. Banish any negative or stagnant energies with your besom or smudge.
2. Call upon your gods, ancestors, guides, and Psychopomp Teacher. Pray to them and ask them to assist you in this healing process.
3. You may stand, sit in a chair, or sit on the ground for this ceremony. I prefer to sit on the floor. I do this because I feel I can connect with the person better. Try different ways and see which one works better for you.
4. Open your heart and fill the room with love and compassion for the person who has died. Summon the spirit by calling the person's name a few times and visualize them appearing before you. See them surrounded by loving divine light. It may to help to visualize the veil between the worlds in order for the spirit to come to you more clearly. If you visualize an energy veil, see the veil opening up to allow the spirit to come forth.
5. Send the energy of balance, calmness, wholeness, and love to the person's heart chakra. You are bringing them into this state to transition in a balanced way.
6. If you perceive any energy chords that are preventing the person from transitioning in a peaceful way, cut them in

your mind so they are no longer causing your person any negative thoughts or emotions. Energy chords that are attached to people, places, things, or circumstances are no longer needed. It is time to let these things go in order to transition in a place of wholeness and balance.

7. Focus on the Soul Star chakra. This is the chakra that connects them to their deity or the Universe in general. If they follow a particular god or goddess, see them dwelling in the Soul Star chakra. If they have no specific god or goddess, you can see a bright light that is the Universe or The Creator. Send energy to the Soul Star chakra and visualize it becoming bright and vibrant.

8. Send bright healing light energy to the Soul Star. Visualize the divine being becoming brighter and brighter. Now, visualize the divine being (or the Universal light) sending loving and compassionate energy down to the spirit making them balanced, whole, and blissful.

9. Visualize the person's spirit absorbing this loving divine energy. It is here that the person is becoming one with the divine. Now, see the person's spirit become very bright as they absorb the energies of the divine. Visualize them becoming wrapped in the energetic love of the divine.

10. Visualize the person's ancestors appearing through a portal from the Land of the Ancestors. See the person reunited with love, joy, and peace.

11. Once you see the person going through the portal into the Land of the Ancestors, cut the energy cord between you and the person.

12. Thank your gods, guides, and Psychopomp Teacher and leave offerings for them.

13. Banish the remaining energies from your work with a besom or smudge.

Blessing of the Body After the Time of Death

There may be times when we are asked to bless the body after someone has died. A body blessing is done in many religions and each religion may have different purposes. A body blessing can be performed to protect the body from negative energies. It can also be blessed to make the body sacred in order to be buried or cremated. I perform body blessings to celebrate and honor the physical body as well as celebrate the spirit of the person who once inhabited the body. A body blessing can be performed by anyone. You do not have to be a priest or priestess in order to do a blessing. In fact, it is highly encouraged that the person's family and close friends perform the body blessing. You can guide them in this process. The family may want you to bless the body and this is something we should do gladly.

After the time of death, the body should be cleaned. Sometimes the family may want to do a symbolic spiritual bath. This can be easily done with a bowl of fresh water and a washcloth. The body should remain draped with a blanket or bedsheet to keep their modesty. The bowl of water can be blessed if you choose but does not have to be. To wash the body, dip the cloth in the water and gently dab the head and face. Then undrape the arm and dip the cloth in the water again and gently stroke down the arm from shoulder to hand. Then repeat with the next arm. Undrape the leg and dip the cloth in the bowl and gently stroke down the leg from hip to foot. You may gently wash the feet as well. Repeat with the second leg. Because the washing is symbolic there is no need to wash the torso or the back.

To bless the body, you take some essential oil and dab on our finger. Any oil that is spiritual and sacred to you will be fine. Place your mind in a sacred place. You are doing holy work. Take a few deep breaths and center yourself. Bring to mind the sacred energies of the moment and the sacred energies of transitioning into death. You can use these words or change them as you like. The important thing is to speak from the heart.

1. Place a drop of oil on the top of the head on the crown and say, **"This is (name)'s connection to spirit. He/She/ They are a child of the gods who walked their path with sacredness."**

2. Place a drop of oil on the brow chakra and say, **"(Name) had many dreams. Many were fulfilled. Some were not. But it was these dreams that gave (name) wonder to look upon the stars."**

3. Place a drop of oil on the throat chakra and say, **"(Name) spoke their truth in whatever form in the best way they could. How they experienced Spirit is what helped shape the truth and the words they spoke."**

4. Place a drop of oil on the heart chakra and say, **"(Name) expressed love in the best way they knew how. He/ She/ They received the love of family and friends in this place of the heart. It is the heart that sees the world. It is the love of (name) that we will remember."**

5. Place a drop of oil on each hand and say, **"These hands are sacred because these are the hands that held our own hands when we needed it. These are the hands and arms that embraced us."**

6. Place a drop of oil on the solar plexus chakra and say, **"(Name) expressed herself/himself/ themselves the best way they knew how. This was once the place of their Will that moved (name) forward. Now we bless this place for a life well lived."**

7. Place a drop on the naval chakra and say, **"(Name) created their world and their universe with each step they took on their path. Each breath they took was a connection to spirit. Now we release their Spirit to transition to a new journey."**

8. Place a drop of oil on either side of the hips and say,

"(Name) walked this earth in love and beauty. Each of her/his/ their steps was a connection to Mother Earth. Now we say goodbye to this physical body but know our loved one walk with love and beauty in the world of spirit."

9. Go back to the head of the body and say, **"This is the sacred vessel of our loved one, (name). This is the body that they used in life to maneuver through the world. This is the body (name) used to love and to be loved. This is the body (name) used to realize her/his/their hopes and dreams. This is the body that gave (name) a life well lived. It is now time for the body to be let go. It will not be needed for the journey ahead. Please join me in moment of silence and prayer for our dear loved one."** Allow a few moments for prayer or meditation for those in attendance.

Chapter 6

Working with the Spirits

I have come to believe that anyone can learn to see and hear the spirits. We all have the magick deep inside ourselves. We just have to figure out the best way to tap into our psychic power to see the spirits. If there is a trick to seeing the spirits, then I would have to say that it is remembering that we are all born with some ability to do so. Think back for a moment to a time when you were a child and your imagination was everything. You could imagine that you could fly, perhaps you were a valiant knight, or maybe you were a wizard or witch who lived deep in the forest and had great powers of magick. Many of us, as children, would imagine adventures with many other characters. Some of these make-believe characters journeyed with us on our great adventures. Other of these characters were the villain that we had to defeat to save the kingdom. For just a moment, allow yourself to believe that maybe these characters were not make-believe at all. Maybe, just maybe, they were actual spirits who enjoyed playing with us.

As I said, I believe we all have the ability to see the spirits. Yes, some magical people are natural seers and do not have to try hard to see the spirits, while the rest of us have to practice daily in order to get just a little hint that the spirits are there. I want to make something very clear; just because it may be difficult for you to see the spirits now, does not mean you will not grow into a powerful seer. Think of it like this: some people can take the flute and make beautiful music while others have to take classes every single day in order to play a melody. Yet, after diligent study both types of people are playing in a world-renowned orchestra. I may have people who disagree with me, but talent may get you started and maybe even a head start, but it is daily practice that makes someone one excel at something. Spirit work is the same way.

You can do psychopomp work without seeing the spirits very clearly, but it will help you in the long run if you continue to cultivate your clairvoyant abilities. By being able to see the spirits as clearly as possible, you will be able to understand and work with them more easily. They will not be able to keep information from you. Sometimes, the spirits are confused, and it is difficult for them to explain why they need your help. First, let me clarify by what I mean to "see" the spirits. There many different levels of perception when it comes to working with the spirits.

Clairvoyance is the psychic ability to see the spirits with your eyes. However, "seeing with your eyes" is kind of a misnomer. You do not actually see them with your physical eyes. The mechanics of clairvoyance is that your mind is able to see the spirit on the astral plane. It does this through the imagination. Remember, your imagination gives the energy that your mind perceives as form and shape so that your everyday consciousness can better understand what your mind is perceiving. Then, your mind projects the image of the spirit in your physical surroundings much like if you were watching a film projector showing a movie on your wall.

Clairaudience is the psychic ability to hear the spirit as well as other sounds such as music, birds, automobiles, etc. This ability is very helpful to the psychopomp because often spirits of the dead want to tell us their story; why and how they died. They also can tell us why they cannot or will not cross over to the afterlife. Many times, students who are beginning to learn to hear the spirits think that it is just voices from their own mind. One of the best ways to find out if you are really hearing the voice of a spirit is to have them tell you something that you do not already know and then verify. While we are learning to see and hear spirits, remember to suspend your disbelief and act as though you really are hearing the spirits. This will help you gain confidence in your psychic work and strengthen your abilities.

Clairsentience is the psychic ability to sense or feel the spirits. Thus the whole, "I can't see you, but I know you're there!" feeling you get when the spirits are around, but you may not be able to see them. Normally, there is a strong feeling of a spiritual presence of some kind. Even people who do not develop their psychic skills are able to sense energies and spirits. When you go to a sacred place, church, temple, or a mountainside you can feel the presence of the sacred. Essentially, this is clairsentience. Remember when you were a kid and you could not see the ghost in the closet, but you definitely felt it there! For me, after my empathic abilities strengthened, this was my second psychic power to develop. I think empathy and clairsentience go hand in hand with each other.

Clairalience is the psychic ability to smell the spirits or other energies. With this skill you will smell scents that belong only to a particular spirit. For example, if you smell a certain brand of perfume that your grandmother wore. Perhaps a spirit you are working with was a mechanic and every time he arrives you smell oil and gasoline. This skill might seem strange, but it comes in quite handy. In the physical world you can often smell scents long before and after a spirit was there. With clairvoyance, you cannot see the spirit until they are in your magical space, but with clairalience you know they are on their way simply from just the scent of them.

Claircognizance is the psychic ability to receive information or have a "knowing" from the spirits. This usually happens when the psychopomp asks the spirit a question and they instantly know the answer. How many times have you said, "I don't know how I know, I just know"? I am convinced that if you are a parent, then you have this ability. Teachers too! This is one of those powers that feels like you may be making it all up in your imagination. That is ok! Just go with it. As we are developing our psychic powers your imagination may sometimes fill in the blank spots. This is perfectly fine. You can verify the information as you need. Whenever I received claircognizant information, I may say to a spirit, "I'm getting that you were a chef in life. Is this correct?" The spirit may clarify with a yes or no answer.

Just as everyone is an individual and everyone learns differently, each of us will develop psychic skills differently. Clairvoyance was probably the last skill I was able to develop and I had to work very hard at it. For me, clairsentience was the easiest, but I still practiced it as often as I could. After much practicing, I was able to practice all the above psychic skills. The reason I tell you this, is because I do not want you to get frustrated if you are having a hard time with any or all of the "clair" skills. You can certainly become a very powerful psychic with practice. In the rest of this chapter, I will help you improve your psychic skills. Just like a seed, your psychic ability simply needs to be watered and given care and diligence to grow into something beautiful.

"A new you comes to light when you engage the power of your spirit. As you expand your circumference of awareness, you begin to participate in the full continuum of life. The physical realm is just one aspect of the vast multidimensional spectrum that we are all a part of."
-Sherrie Dillard, *You Are a Medium: Discover Your Natural Abilities to Communicate With the Otherside.*

The Ancestors

The best way to begin with learning how to work with the spirits is through honoring your ancestors. Over many years of training students to work with the spirits of the dead, I have found that if we start with our own ancestors, the student's clairvoyant skills advance at a much quicker rate. It is always better to work with spirits that care about our wellbeing in the beginning before we seek out spirits that we do not know. Our own ancestors have a special bond with us that no other spirit has. They are our family and they love us and want to see us succeed. Unlike other spirits, our ancestors are patient and look forward to our spiritual development. The more our psychic abilities grow the more the ancestors will be able to communicate with us. The ancestors are already communicating with us even if we know it or not. They may talk with us in dreams or pop in our minds during the holidays and stressful times in our lives. Have you ever been going through some life challenges and thought, "If only so and so were here, they would know what to do." Then suddenly you felt the comfort of that memory and found the advice you needed within yourself. This is but one way that the ancestors connect with us.

It is my hope that anyone who calls themselves a pagan, witch, or Spirit Walker honors their ancestors on a daily basis. The Universe is made up of the three shamanic worlds and if we are only honoring the gods, then we are only honoring one third of the spiritual beings who can help us on our spiritual path. There are many reasons we should honor our ancestors. First and foremost, they are our family. Even though family can have their problems, they are still there for each other. No one has a perfect family. There are many things about families that are challenging, but family is family and family is the most important thing. When our loved ones cross into the Land of the Ancestors, they do not forget about us. They love us through space and time and will help us in whatever way they can. If you ask them, they will be delighted to walk side by side with you on our spiritual path.

In many pagan traditions, the ancestors are called upon so that they may attend our ceremonies. They are our honored guests. The ancestors are our strongest link between us living human beings and the spirits who dwell in the otherworlds.

They are our biggest advocate and will stand by us as we traverse into the realms of spirit. When we ask the gods for help, they have to consider the greater good of the Universe. Sometimes the magick that we conjure is for our own personal betterment and may not necessarily help our community. The gods have to weigh the greater good of everyone before they allow your magick to manifest. The ancestors are only concerned about you and your wellbeing. You will always be part of their lineage. That will never change. They are not so much concerned about the greater good of the community and you and your family will always come first. So, it is better to work magick with your ancestors to be able to obtain some of the outcomes you desire.

When honoring our ancestors becomes a daily spiritual practice, our psychic abilities will begin to develop much faster than they would otherwise. Many years ago, when I first started working with my ancestors, I could not see nor hear them. I was able to sense them, so I knew they were there energetically. Each day I would light my ancestor candle and pray for their wellbeing. I would speak with them about my day and intuit their energy the best I could with my heart. Eventually, I began to hear and see them in my mind. Over weeks and months of talking with my ancestors and being open to whatever spiritual expression in which they chose to manifest, I began to see spiritual energies more clearly. Eventually, I was able to see my ancestors appear in my home and in ritual. Not only was I able to see my beloved dead, but my skills to see all spirits greatly improved. I was able to see the gods, nature spirits, and many other energies very clearly. I can attest, that the ancestors do help you develop the ability to see and hear spirits.

Our ancestors are a particularly important part of our psychopomp work. Not only are they able to help us to see and hear the spirits, they can help us work with them as well. The ancestors have the ability to travel wherever they like in the Underworld and the Land of the Ancestors. Like all spirits, they can travel anywhere at the speed of thought. When you are helping a spirit cross over to the afterlife, it is vitally important that their ancestors assist in this process. The spirit who is earthbound will most likely be suffering in some way. They could be angry, confused, or lost in their own sadness and melancholy. They will feel more comfortable crossing into the portals that leads to the afterlife if they have loving and compassionate ancestor to help facilitate their journey home. Many spirits who are earthbound refuse to cross over, so it will take some convincing for them to leave the physical plane. No one knows the earthbound person like their ancestors do. Even if they are relatives that the person never met in life, they will still have a loving energetic connection. The earthbound spirit will be able to feel this and will feel more comfortable going with them through the portal that leads them home.

Working with Your Ancestors

Connecting to our family is something many of us do daily even if it is only in our thoughts. It is equally important to connect with our ancestors every single day. Before doing great works of magick with the ancestors you must establish a relationship with them. This relationship must progress naturally and the bond between you must grow. You cannot rush spiritual growth, but you can nurture it so that it becomes strong and everlasting. The first thing you will need to do to start working with the ancestors is to build an ancestor altar in your home. I have a detailed description on how to build an ancestral altar in my book *Deeper Into The Underworld: Death, Ancestors, and Magical Rites,* but I will give you an abridged version here. If you would like to check out more details do, indeed, check out the book.

The first thing you will need to do is decide which of your ancestors you would like to honor. Some people have the privilege of knowing who your ancestors were for many generations. The rest of us are not so lucky. My advice is to do some digging. Ask your older relatives about who your ancestors were. Sometimes a family bible may have a few generations of family members written down. Also, you will be surprised about who's family photo album has pictures of relatives long forgotten. You also have the websites *23andme.com* and *Ancestors.com* to help you. I actually found several ancestors using these sites. The drawback is that someone in your extended family needs to fill in the family tree. So, if no one does that then you will be at a loss. These websites can also help you connect to second and third cousins who may have information about your ancestors. Again, start by asking your parents, grandparents, cousins, aunts, and uncles about where your family comes from. If it is possible, get the birth and death dates as well. Hopefully, you will discover several of your ancestors.

To begin your ancestor work you will need to start with three or four ancestors. If you have found more than three or four, then you get to decide who is best for your spiritual work. In order to decide, look over each ancestor's picture (or just the name if there is no photo) and try to visualize each one as clearly as possible. Ask them in your heart if they would like to work with you on your altar. If you get the intuition that it is a good match, then you may place them on your altar. If it is unclear or you are not getting a good energetic reading, then you can use your pendulum to tap into their energy and ask them if they would like to be on your ancestral altar. Do not be offended if the answer is no. They may have other work they are doing in the spirit world, or perhaps their energies are not congruent to your work as a psychopomp. Either way, always respect their wishes.

The next thing you will need to do is find a small table or bookshelf that will act as an ancestral altar. As long as the table holds items needed to create the altar, any type will do. It needs to be placed where the family spends most of the time such as a living room, dining room, or perhaps the kitchen. The reason for this is because we need to treat all of our spirits like they are welcomed guests. There are some cases where someone might have roommates and it is easier to do their spiritual work in the privacy of the bedroom. In this case, I would make sure to explain to the ancestors that they are welcome anywhere in the home. Place each picture you have of your ancestors in a picture frame. If you cannot find a picture of one of your ancestors, leave the frame empty or have a black background and use it as a magick mirror for your ancestor to come through. You should also place mementos of your ancestors on the altar if you have them. If you do not have any mementos, that is ok. They are not necessary but do add to the energies. You will need one large central candle for the altar. The flame will give them energy as well as act as a symbol to tell your consciousness that the ancestors are present. In front of each picture you will need to place a small bowl or glass for water. The water also gives them energy as well as acts a portal for the ancestors to come through. Anytime you have water or a mirror it is a portal into the Underworld. This is one of the reasons wells are sacred. You can also place religious statues, pictures, or icons on the altar if all your ancestor practiced the same religion. If they are all different religions, then do not place anything extra on the altar. The setup of the ancestral altar should look like this:

1. Three to four picture frames each containing a picture of your ancestor. If no picture, you can leave it blank.
2. Place any mementos you may have of each ancestor near their picture.
3. One small bowl or glass in front of each picture.
4. One central candle.
5. Any religious statues, pictures, or icons – if appropriate.

Once your altar is set up you will be ready to begin. Stand in front of the ancestor altar and visualize your ancestors in your heart. Try to tune in to their energies the best you can. While you visualize, send them the energies of love and compassion. When you are ready, light your central candle and pray to the gods for them to grant blessing upon your ancestors. It is always better to say what is in your heart, but you can say something like, "I ask the gods to grant blessings upon my ancestors. I ask that my ancestors (name), (name), and (name) receive peace, healing, and spiritual evolution." Make sure you say each of their names. When you do this, it gives special attention to each of them. Then tell your ancestors about your day and what is going on with your family. The ancestors will always be interested in how the family is doing. You can pour them each a fresh glass of water as an offering. This will give them energy as well as strengthen your connection between them and you.

Offerings to the Ancestors

From time to time you should give your ancestors food offerings. I do not do this every day, but I try to do it whenever I can. Once every week or so should be fine. It is also important to do on birthdays and holidays as well. Different pagan traditions will have different practices when it comes to food offerings. If you follow a certain tradition with requirements about offerings, then it is a good idea to follow the instructions of your tradition. I have been honoring the ancestor for quite some time and I will give you the procedures that I have found helpful.

Each ancestor should have their own small dish for the food offering. You can have one large plate for everyone, but I found they feel a bit more special if you allow them their own dish. The amount is up to you. I usually either give them a few tablespoons or enough to fill the small dish. Spirits do not need to eat as much as we do. When you give the ancestors offerings, always serve them first before you serve the living or the gods. After all, they are your guests. Food offerings can be just about anything. You can give them meat, but I would make sure it is always cooked. I would not serve anyone raw meat. That is just gross; never mind the taboos against feeding the dead blood. Make sure your food does not have a lot of salt in it. As you know, salt is very grounding for energy, and it is very depleting for the ancestors to try to draw energy from it. On special occasions you can give them small glass of alcohol and cigarettes if you choose. One thing to remember is that if your ancestor was an alcoholic in life, they may still carry those addictions in death. It is better to just serve water, juice, or milk if that is the case. You can usually discard the food offering the next day. The spirits will take out the life force of the food so it will usually be old and dry by the morning. How you discard the offerings is up to you. You can put them in a compost or place in the earth. It is also perfectly acceptable if you throw them in the trash. In my experience, the food has been drained of vital force, so it is not good for animals to eat. Not because it has the energy of death or anything like that, but because the life force of the offering is gone.

Strengthening the Connection

In the beginning, when working with the ancestors, it may seem quiet with little interaction from your ancestors. You will be developing psychic skills that you may not have used before so I would like you to be very patient with yourself and your ancestors during this process. You cannot rush good results. This is one of those times in magick and spirituality that slow and steady does truly win the race. With persistence, your psychic skills will grow many times more powerful that you will imagine. The most important thing is daily practice. By being consistent in your daily work you will strengthen the connection with our ancestors and in turn you will develop stronger psychic skills.

To begin, light your ancestor candle and say your prayer for the ancestors. Visualize the ancestors in your heart. Imagine what their energies feel like. Do not worry about doing it correctly or not. Open your heart and spend some time thinking about what the energies of your beloved family in spirit would feel like. See them in your heart and fill your heart with love. Your ancestors will feel the love you have for them. This gives them energetic strength and will deepen your connection with them. As you talk to them about your day and what is happening with your family, pour the water in their water bowls. Make sure that every single time you are doing a meditation, magical techniques, rituals, or spells, that you are inviting them to attend. Allow them to contribute to the energies if they choose. After a few weeks of this, when you light the ancestor candle and say your prayer to them, you will start to feel their presence in your home. This is when we psychically start to feel the spirits. This is the *clairsentience* part of your development. You may not be able to hear or see them, but you can feel them. For most magical folk, clairsentience is one of the first abilities we develop. We magical people tend to feel many energies at the same time and the ancestor's energies may be drowned out by other energies you are perceiving. Spend some time trying to feel them. Remember the feeling of them in your heart? Tune in to that feeling in your home. They are certainly there; we may just need to adjust our energy sensing abilities to them. After I learned to do this, I tried to sense the different energies of the spirits I would call in rituals and spells. Every spirit has a different feel to them. I call this their energy signature. If you are having trouble sensing them, open your heart chakra and expand your Sphere of Sensation. This will allow you to sense the spirits in the room a lot better.

After a few more weeks of this, your psychic abilities will begin to develop further, and you will be able to hear or smell the ancestors as well as sense them. For me, I was able to smell spiritual scents before I was able to hear them. This is the *clairalience* progression of your powers. I remember sensing my ancestors in the room and suddenly smelling my grandmother's perfume. By smelling her perfume, this just solidified that I was doing it right! It made me more confident that the spirits were responding to the work I was doing. The funny thing is, that it did not stop there. I could smell distinct scents for my gods, the faeries, and any other spirit. One of the benefits I had found with the power of clairalience is that I could smell the spirits long before a witch could see the spirit. You know how you can smell someone's strong perfume before they enter the room? Same thing with smelling spiritual aromas.

For some people, the ability to hear the voices of the ancestors comes before the ability to smell scents. For others, it may come after. Just like how we all learn differently; we also experience psychic abilities at different points in our development. Our brains are just wired differently. Also, there is something to be said about receiving a magical gift when your mind is ready to believe that it is possible to perform. During our daily prayers for the ancestors we should be talking to them every single day. By telling them about our day and of what is happening to our family, we are including them in our lives and continuing to create stronger energetic links to the ancestors. Our words have power. If we look at the mechanics of how our words have magick, we can see that the vibrations of our voice become a conduit for our intent, energy, and our emotions. Essentially, this is how chants and sacred music cause change in the astral as well as the physical plane. Our voices can be heard into the depths of the spirit worlds.

Each time you speak with your ancestors, imagine that they are responding back to you. I suggest starting this process a few weeks or so after you begin the lighting of your ancestral candle and talking to them. Once you are able to sense their energies in your home, imagine what they would say if you *could* hear them. At this point, do not get caught up in the idea that it is just all in your mind. For now, just go with it. What we are doing is training your consciousness to be ready to hear the voices of the ancestors once your psychic abilities strengthen to the point of *clairaudience*. What I learned to do, is that while speaking to my ancestors I sense their energies and emotions. Then I would intuit their answers and put that into words in my mind. You might get it wrong, but you might get it right. If you would like confirmation, you can use the pendulum and ask them if what your imagination intuited and heard was correct. If not, do not worry. You will improve over time. The ancestors are patient with your mistakes and are very much willing to wait until you can hear them well enough for a conversation. At first, you may only hear muffled sounds or sounds that seem far away. This is great! This means that you are strengthening your clairaudience abilities and you are on your way to clear hearing! Over time, using this approach, you will be able to hear them as clear as day. Just keep talking to them and intuiting what their words would be.

By now, you have been lighting your ancestral candle and saying your prayers for them. You have been telling them about your day and your family. While doing this, you are sensing the presence of the ancestors in your home and paying attention to any scents you may smell linking them to your ancestors. You have also been intuiting what they are telling you and putting it into words with your imagination in your mind. When you put this all together, you are ready to go to the next phase of your psychic abilities – seeing the ancestors, or what we call *clairvoyance*. Seeing the ancestors, or any spirit, is a lot easier than you may think. What we have to do is acknowledge the little steps that it takes to achieve the goal of psychic sight.

Your imagination and visualization skills are the cornerstone to seeing the spirits. Many of us have asked ourselves at one time or another "am I making this all up?". The answer is "Yes you are!" But that is exactly what you are supposed to do. Remember that everything in the Universe is energy. Energy comes in waves, pulses, flashes, and particles. It is extremely difficult to have a conversation with the energy flashes. It would be like having a conversation with a disco light. Very difficult at best. Your mind needs to put the energy in a tangible form so it can converse with it just as it does physical things. Your mind should visualize a form or shape, so it is easier to communicate with. In essence, you are visualizing what your ancestors look like in your mind in order to give them form. Over time, as your connection to your ancestors continues to strengthen, your mind will begin to give your ancestors form outside of your mind. When observing the ancestors in your home your mind will superimpose your ancestors on to the physical plane much like how an old movie projector will project a scene on to the wall. This is one of reasons why spirits seem to have a translucent appearance; you are seeing their astral form as it appears in your mind.

While you are first learning to sense and hear the spirits, you may start to see colors, symbols, or shapes in your mind. In the beginning of learning clairvoyance, this is how your imagination is trying to find the form most appropriate to the ancestor energy you are perceiving. My advice is to help your imagination by visualizing what you think the ancestors look like by the pictures you have on your altar. If one or more of your ancestors has no photo, then allow your imagination to come up with what you think your ancestors look like based off what you are feeling with your clairsentient abilities. In other words, how do you think they will appear based off how they feel to you. What some people do when they are learning to see the ancestors is to place a magick mirror on the ancestor altar. With the magick mirror you can scry into the astral plane in order to see what they look like.

A psychic ability that will especially develop differently for each person is the power of *claircognizance*. As it pertains to the ancestors, this is when you just *know* things. You may ask your ancestors questions about their life and, without them speaking to you, you will know the answer. Sometimes this is telepathy, but most of the time it is your psychic ability to retrieve the answer you are searching for from the cosmic web of the Universe. The magical science behind this is that your Sphere of Sensation is connecting to the Cosmic Web and information is given to you freely. It is almost like you are plugged directly into the mainframe of the Universe. This comes in handy because you will just know things about your ancestors without putting much effort into it. For me, this ability came before I was able to see spirits. But again, it is different for everyone. I had a magical friend for whom this was his first psychic ability and everything else came after.

Like I said before, we all learn and experience things differently. How your psychic abilities manifest will be as unique as you are. What is presented here is the most common manifestation of psychic abilities for the students whom I have taught. You may or may not experience these psychic abilities in the order they are presented in this work, but it really does not matter in what order these abilities appear. The important thing is that you continue to strengthen your connection to the ancestors so you may have a loving and healing relationship with your ancestors.

Journeying with the Ancestors

One of the most powerful ways to work with your beloved dead is to journey in spirit to the Land of the Ancestors. Journeying in spirit and astral projection are pretty much the same thing. They both use trance techniques to help your spirit (or astral body) to leave your physical body in order to explore the three shamanic worlds. The differences are more cultural than anything else. Journeying in spirit, sometimes called shamanic journeying, is an indigenous technique while astral projection was made popular by ceremonial magicians. It is important to journey to the Underworld and the Land of the Ancestors because it will further our connections with our family in the spirit world. When we are calling our ancestors to our home, we are asking them to come and visit us. When we journey to them in spirit, we are going to them. Think of it this way, we should go and visit our family's home just as we ask them to come and visit our home. It is a form of energy exchange and also politeness.

One of the benefits of journeying to the ancestors is that you will be able to deepen the practice of your psychic abilities. Just as you use your imagination to visualize and hear the spirits, you will use your imagination to journey to the Underworld. Once again, it is our imagination that allows the abstract energies of the spirits to take form so we can better communicate with them. The practice of spirit journeying is quite simple. All you need to do is use the power of your mind and visualization skills, and you will be transported to a land of beauty, healing, and wellbeing. While you are in the Land of the Ancestors it is important to practice your "clair" abilities. By visualizing your ancestors with your imagination, you are using clairvoyance. By imagining what they are saying and what they sound like, you are using clairaudience. By using your heart and Sphere of Sensation and sensing them, you are using clairsentience. By smelling the beautiful environment of the afterlife as well as any perfume or cologne, they may be wearing, you are using clairalience.

It will be very special to your family in spirit when you visit them in the afterlife. It takes little effort to journey to them and they will feel appreciated and loved. Remember, your family loves you and by journeying to them it will only deepen both your bond with your ancestors as well as your psychic ability.

Journeying to the Land of the Ancestors is extremely easy. If you like, you can make this into a full ceremony, or you can do the technique on its own.

Journey to Your Ancestors

1. Light your ancestral altar candle and explain to your ancestors that you are going to journey to the Land of the Ancestors to see them.

2. You may sit or lie down for this exercise. If you like, you may play music and light incense. Any incense that makes you feel otherworldly and magical with do.

3. Take a few deep breaths and place yourself in light trance. Focus on the work that is to be done at this time.

4. State aloud your purpose to the spirits. You should speak from your heart, but you can say something like, **"I seek to journey to the Land of the Ancestors with my Psychopomp Teacher in order to connect with my ancestors."**

5. Close your eyes and visualize your Psychopomp Teacher standing before you. Ask them to guide you through the Land of the Ancestors.

6. Visualize a portal to the afterlife opening in your magical space. Your Psychopomp Teacher will guide you into the portal.

7. When you arrive in the ancestral lands, your ancestors should be awaiting your arrival. If not, open your heart chakra and call out to them. Visualize them appearing before you.

8. Spend some time with your ancestors. Ask them to show you where they live and what their lives are like. Take all the time you need. Try using your clair abilities in your journey.

9. When you are ready to return, say your goodbyes and visualize the portal back to the physical plane opening up. Go back through the portal and see yourself back at home.

10. When you are ready, take a deep breath and bring yourself back into your physical body.

11. Center and ground as needed. Journal your experiences.

A Seance

Once you have practiced your new psychic abilities, it is time to put them into practice. A seance. I can only imagine your thoughts when you saw this section titled "Seance". I bet you are imagining people dressed up in Victorian garb holding hands around a tipping table or a Ouija board asking spirits to flicker the lights or make a knocking sound. These things can certainly be in a seance session, but they do not have to be. My magical spiritual work is always focused around reconnection to Spirit and healing. So, for this last section of this chapter I would like to have you use the skills you have learned so far and put them into practice. After all, in order to do effective psychopomp work you need to be able to see, hear, and sense the spirits to the best of your ability. Also, you need to make sure you are continually practicing your clair skills. We would not want you to get rusty before a spirit of the dead asks you for help in crossing the veil into the afterlife.

We are going to perform an old fashioned seance but with some modern additions so that we are performing a ceremony with the energies of healing and spiritual growth.

With all things magical, I ask that you have an open mind as we work with the spirits of the dead and do our best to practice our psychic abilities. You can certainly perform this ceremony alone, but I have found, while you are still learning, it is best to perform this with two or more people. Partly, because it can be jarring if spirit phenomenon occurs and having someone with you will ease any tensions. Also, the more people you have the stronger the energy and magick will be. If you choose to have other people with you, make sure they are magical people; or at least open to your spiritual experimentation.

Set Up - To set up for your seance ceremony, I suggest using a small table draped with black cloth. If you do not have black cloth handy that is ok. You will want to have one white candle at the center of the table and perhaps some incense. Any incense that makes you feel magical will do. In tradition, herbs such as sage, mugwort, wormwood, copal, or dittany of Crete are good for calling the spirits. The room should be dark. You can certainly do this during the day if need be, but I prefer nighttime. After all, the night is the time of the witches. If you are alone, place your hands directly on the table. If you have more than one person, each of you should hold hands and create an energy circuit. You do not have to hold hands the entire time only at the beginning.

Prayers to the Gods, Guides and Psychopomp Teacher - To start your seance ceremony, say a prayer to your gods, spirit guides, and Psychopomp Teacher. Praying to them from the heart is the most powerful and genuine way to begin. Ask them to add power to your ceremony, protect you from harm, and guide the participants as you proceed.

Protection: Visualize White Light - As you hold hands, visualize powerful healing white light emanating from the white candle in a beautiful sphere. See the sphere of light growing larger and larger. As it expands, it banishes any spirit that is not beneficial for the ceremony.

Statement of Purpose - State your purpose of your ceremony aloud. You may say something to the effect of, "Tonight we seek to communicate with the spirits of the dead for spiritual growth and healing."

Energy Healing Meditation - Have someone lead an energy healing mediation. This helps to balance your energies and also place you in a light trance for the work a head. A nice simple meditation is to breath in the light of the Universe and have it enter your chakras. Start with the crown, brow, throat, heart, solar plexus, naval, and root. See the energy balance and brighter each chakra.

Calling to the Spirit - Everyone should now open their brow and heart chakras as well as expand their Sphere of Sensation to encompass the entire room. Each person should send out compassionate and healing energy. The spirits will feel this energy and feel at ease. Call out to the spirits. You can say something like, "We invite anyone who would like to communicate with us to make themselves known. We seek to better understand you. Speak to our minds and our hearts."

Using Your Psychic Skills - This is the time to use all the psychic skills you have learned throughout this chapter. With your Sphere of Sensation try to sense the spirits in the room (clairsentience). Using this feeling allow your imagination to shape these energies into form and see what the spirits look like (clairvoyance). Now with the feeling and form established, try to hear what they are saying the best you can (clairaudience). You can seek further information by checking for the scents from the spirits (clairalience). Also do not be surprised with the information you just seem to know (claircognizance). Allow plenty of time for everyone to perceive the spirits to the best of their ability. What information would you like to know about the spirits? If you are having trouble seeing the spirits on this particular occasion you may use a magick mirror or scrying bowl, but the goal is to communicate with them without devices.

Thanks - Once you are ready to end your seance ceremony, give thanks to the spirits who spoke with you.

Thanking Gods, Guides and Psychopomp Teacher - Thank

your gods, spirit guides, and your Psychopomp Teacher for their help and guidance with your ceremony. Leave offerings to them as a thank you.

Cleansing - You should do a cleansing after you have completed the ritual. You do not want any negative energies or trickster spirits appearing who are attracted to your ritual. You can visualize a sphere of cleansing light encompassing the room or you can use a formal cleansing ceremony if you have one. Journal your experience.

Chapter 7

Earthbound

The Earthbound Dead

At the time of death, a person becomes free of their physical body and is able to move around and journey into the Land of the Ancestors. They are free of physical pain and the restraints of the earthly plane. An energetic portal or door opens and out step the ancestors, gods, and guardian spirits that the person knew in life. Even if the person did not have a spiritual practice, they will often recognize their ancestors. They may see their parents, grandparents, partners, and friends. There is a strong feeling of love in the room. The person feels safe and loved. There is nothing to fear. Through the energy portal is a place of love and welcoming. The Land of the Ancestors. All will be well. The ancestors take them by the hand and lovingly guide them to a magical place of healing and sacred community. But what if death comes to a person in a way that is tragic and unexpected? What if at the point of death there is so much chaos and confusion that the energy of love is not felt? What if at death, there are more important things that need to be taken care of so the afterlife must wait until another time?

We are often taught by many spiritual leaders that, during the transition of death, our loved ones are taken to a place of love and light and there is nothing for us to worry or be sad about. All is well. In reality, we know that the world is much more complex than this. When we see the news reports from all over the world, we see that there are many instances of war, starvation, poverty, crime, hate, and abuse. Many people die every single day because of these things. As I said before, when someone dies, they retain their hopes, dreams, fears, and prejudices. When they died, they may have had plans unfulfilled, children to take care of, or even a score to settle. Their bodies are damaged beyond repair, but their spirits remain unchanged. There are many reasons why the spirits of the dead remain bound to the Earth. Sometimes they have a great purpose for remaining on the physical plane. Sometimes they are simply confused. They are in emotional and energetic pain and are not sure what to do. Other times, they feel that they have a great purpose to remain close to Earth, so they refuse to cross over. When we are energetically healing the dead and guiding them to the afterlife, it is important to try to have as much compassion and empathy for them as we can. We are called to do this work because we care about others. To do the work of the psychopomp effectively and lovingly, we should try to understand the reasons they are earthbound as best as we can.

In the following pages, I will share some of the stories from just a few of the spirits I have helped heal and guided to the afterlife. Each of these people had a unique situation that kept them bound to the earthly plane. As you read each of these stories, I would like you to open your heart and try to empathize with their stories the best you can. It is the healer's open heart and compassion that allows us to understand and connect to each person. This is where the real healing is. Energy healing and escorting the spirit to the afterlife is wonderful but it is in the compassion that we have for each person where the healing begins. Some of the stories are tragic and may be hard to read. In your psychopomp work many of the spirits you encounter will have tragic stories. Honor your feelings for that moment but then put them aside so you can focus on the work at hand. Every person deserves to be heard. Each person deserves to tell their story.

Sudden Death

I don't remember really. The crash, I mean. I remember opening my eyes and the car was totaled. I remember thinking that my dad's gonna be pissed. I'm 16 and I just got my license a little while ago. He's always saying to be careful and drive slowly. I was being careful. Eyes on the road, just like he said. I was just changing the radio station for a second. Seriously! A second! Then I woke up. I got out of the car and looked at the totaled hood and I started walking. I wasn't sure what I should do. I should find a phone and call my parents. Mmmmmmmm... He's gonna be so mad. I was just walking down the street to find a pay phone. The wreck just happened... I think. Yeah, like a minute or so ago. It's weird because I think I've been walking on this road a long time. I think. I keep walking by people. They don't seem to notice me. Where's that phone? My dad's gonna be so mad. I realized something though...I can move my body around in weird ways. Like, I can displace my jaw and if I focus real hard, I can freak people out. Gave one guy a scare! But I just need to find a payphone... My dad's gonna be really mad. Can you help me find a phone? Maybe call my dad?

When we are healthy, no one expects to die so soon. Younger people often feel like they are going to live forever. Or at least for a long time. In our modern day, we have the hustle and bustle of everyday life. We have school, work, family, friends, and many other things that take up the majority of our time every day. We have our goals, hopes, and dreams for the future. Many times, we often focus on the future rather than what we are doing at the moment. It is always the future that will be better. If only we could graduate school, get a new job, or make more money, then our lives will be better than they are now. When someone suddenly dies, there is no more future in this world. Everything that that person wanted to accomplish, every goal, and every dream, will not happen. Physical life is over.

When someone dies unexpectedly, it can be very traumatic. Sudden death can happen by a fatal car accident, surgery, fires, workplace accidents, falls, heart attacks, and many other things.

With the healing work of helping to heal the spirits of the dead, I have found that many of the spirits I help do not even realize that they are dead. You may be asking yourself, "How can you not know you are dead?" Well, denial is a big part of it. Your mind is powerful, and the mental denial of an event is very powerful as well. The shock of their own sudden death can energetically bind the spirit to the earthly plane. Sudden death happens very quickly. So quickly, in fact, that there may not be any pain or the realization that death is imminent. We have all heard of people who mentally create their own reality when there is psychological trauma. When sudden death occurs, it can very well have a great impact on someone's psychological frame of mind and cause trauma. Psychologically they create a "make believe" world. In the spirit world, the dead are no longer bound by the physical plane so they can quite literally create their own world. When this happens, they are not aware of it. They may perceive the world in a way they wish and ignore the fact that the "outside" world is not interacting with them the way it once did.

Violent Death

Right here on this corner. That's where the bastard shot me. Right here on this fucking corner. I was coming back from that club right over there. Do you see it? Right by the elevated train tracks. I had so much fun dancing, drinking, and hanging out with friends. I was getting tired, so I wanted to go home. Maybe get some food on the way. I left my friends there and I was gonna get a cab. Then this fucker comes out of nowhere. I don't even remember him telling me to give him my wallet or anything. Maybe he did. I don't remember. It happened so fast! This guy rushes me and the next thing I know is, I'm shot. And I fall to the ground. That son of a bitch fucking killed me! Fuck! I want him to pay! He ended my life and I want that motherfucker to fucking pay! Fuck jail! Someone needs to fucking shoot him in the nuts. I'm not leaving until the fuck-wad is done! I want him to go down. I will

stay right here and make sure that happens. I ain't going nowhere.
Not until someone takes that fucker down.

When someone dies from sudden death, there is shock and sadness for a future that will never happen. When someone dies from violence, not only is it a future that will never happen, but there can be anger and confusion because the death was not supposed to happen in the minds of the victims. On a greater spiritual scale, we can easily justify all deaths by saying that it was "their time to go". For the victim of a violent death, that is never a satisfying answer. At certain times, the victim of a violent death will be unaware that they have died, especially if it happened quickly. For some victims, they are aware of the trauma and horror that was happening to them that caused their death. When the attack was taking place the mental and emotional trauma can build up to such a great extreme that the energies become powerful enough to bind the person to the earthly plane. This does not mean that every person who dies from violence is earthbound. Not at all. Some may either choose to be here until justice is served or they are unwilling to cross over to the spirit world while their anger and rage keeps them here. For the victims of war, they may choose to stay on the physical plane until the war is over. For them, that is their closure. Please understand that the scenarios I describe here are from my experience and there may be other reasons people who died of violence stay here. I am relating my experience. I am sure you will find different reasons for different people in your experience with psychopomp work.

Addiction

I know it's dark in here sometimes. That's fine, though. I like it
sometimes. Not to be seen. No one knows I'm here. No one knows what
I'm doing. They used to bother me. People telling me to get clean.
They sent me to rehab once. I didn't want to give it up. Not the only

thing that made me feel...normal. That made me feel alive. The only time I felt connected with something. I used to come to this place when I was alive. Oh, yes, I am very aware I'm dead. I don't know how long. I can't really tell. People of all sorts come to this place to get high. To feel a sense of...well, to feel something. Some people come here, and they have old dirty clothes. Probably something someone gave them. Some people come here, and they look spick and span clean. All types, I guess. It's the energy here I like. Oh, yes. It's better than what I used to do. I used to put a needle in my arm. But now, all I have to do is absorb the high. Yes, when people get high, they give off a lot of high energy. I just stand near them and absorb it; and I get to feel the way I should feel. Sometimes, if the energy isn't good enough, I can touch them and get their energy too. Yeah, I can get the high and a little taste of life. They are so high; they don't even know it's happening. If they get sick, I just wait for another one to come along. I know it's dark in here sometimes. I like it.

When someone dies because of an addiction they are sometimes earthbound because of the addictive nature. When someone is an addict, they are often looking for something to fill a great craving. Many times, but not always, addiction is caused by those who are seeking healing in some way. The term *The Self-Medication Hypothesis* was established in 1985. It has come to mean someone who takes substances in order to alleviate symptoms of illness. In their article "Recognizing Forms of Self-Medication", Stephanie Faris and Kathryn Watson write: "The hypothesis claims that people use substances as a response to mental illness. It states that alcohol and drug abuse is often a coping mechanism for people with a variety of mental health conditions, including depression." There are many reasons why someone may become an addict, but energetically speaking, the addict is seeking something outside of themselves that will bring a specific desired result. Every addict is different, but some of the common desired results are happiness, escape, healing, pain relief, and balance. One does not have to be addicted to drugs to be considered an addict. There are many people who are substance free who have addictive behaviors.

It is important to understand that just because the spirit was an addict in some way, it does not necessarily mean they are or will be earthbound. Just as with all earthbound spirits, there are other factors involved. I am presenting a simplistic view of a complicated spiritual matter to get the student of energy healing a place to begin from. When an addict dies, especially because of substance abuse, they will continue to seek their "high" even after death. In Tibetan Buddhism, the term *hungry ghosts* refer to the spirits of the dead who are always hungry because in life they were consumed by greed, jealousy, or addiction. These spirits are always looking for something to satisfy them, but nothing seems to take away their cravings. This is why they are called the hungry ghosts. These spirits of the dead often stay inside or near places where drugs and drug users can be found. They will sometimes attach themselves to a living addict so they may feed off of their high as well as their life force. Spiritually, the addicted spirit is not interested in crossing over to the realm of the ancestors. This can be because they want to be in a place where they can get their energy high. It can also be because they are afraid of being judged by their ancestors and their deities. They may not even believe in an afterlife at all.

Unfinished Business

I've worked so hard on this store. I worked almost every single day making it what it is. I went from having nothing to this store. It's not big like Sears or Macy's, but It's mine. There's so much that has to get done. Every single day I make sure it all gets done. My sons' are doing the best they can ever since I passed, but they don't have my experience. They don't have my know how. I'm watching how they do things. They are trying their best, but I need to stick around to help them. Plus, I have grandchildren now. Little ones, you know.

A boy, eight, and a little girl, six. They play here in the store all the time. One day the store will be theirs. Well, if my boys don't run it into the ground. I gotta make sure they do the right thing. I tell them sometimes what to do and they do it! No, they can't hear me. Not really. They're not psychic either. I just tell them what to do; how to manage the store, and they do it. I don't know how it works, but it works. I work on things in the store here and there. Just little things. They probably don't even notice, but it needs to get done. I can't leave until I know the store is in good hands.

Unfinished business is perhaps one of the more common reasons that the dead do not cross over to be with the ancestors. In the United States, we tend to work ourselves to the bone. We fill our days and free time, not only with our careers, but with many other projects as well. We do not take the time off to rest like we should. We are taught to feel guilty or feel like a failure if we are not constantly working on something. Even in alternative spirituality, we are often taught that to become more evolved and spiritual we should constantly work on our inner self, meditating, honoring the gods, and our own healing. Even in healing we are working.

There are many things that spirits of the dead can consider unfinished business. Not everyone's unfinished business is the same. It could be a lifelong career or business that the spirit wants to keep going. It could be to help people in need. It could also be taking care of family members who may or may not need the help of others. It does not matter if the unfinished business seems unimportant to you. If it is important to the spirit, then it is important enough to keep their spirit from crossing over. As I have said before, when someone dies, they still have free will. They are not forced to walk with their ancestors and deities if they are not ready. If they truly feel that whatever they left behind is unfinished, then they can be bound to the physical plane either until the business is completed in some way or they realize that their work is done and they can move on.

Guardians and Protectors

We were so happy when I became pregnant. She was our first and I had never been happier. I was not one of those girls who was obsessed with babies. But, when I became pregnant, I guess I was a little obsessed. I did all the right things. Doctor appointments, vitamins, exercise, no alcohol, of course. Everything was going well. When I went into labor, something wasn't right. It was a feeling, I guess. I just knew. When we got to the hospital and the doctor examined me and the baby, she said we would have to do a cesarean. It was going to be fine. The doctors know what they are doing. I barely remember going under. It seemed like a moment had passed and then I was floating above my own body. Doctors and nurses seemed frantic. There was so much blood. I was gone. My body was gone. My little girl would be alone. No. No. She needs me. My husband is wonderful, but he can't do this alone. He can't. No. I'm here now. Yes, I've been gone for quite some time now. I'm her guardian angel. I was with her when she learned to walk. I was with her all through school and I am with her now she has a child of her own. She's making too many mistakes. I wasn't there in the flesh to show her, so I have to do it for her now. Who else is going to help her? I've learned to throw diapers on the floor when she should change her baby. I can even break things if I need to. I have had a long time to practice. She has me if she wants me or not. I'm here for her. She can't do it on her own.

Our energetic bonds to our loved ones are very powerful. When someone dies leaving children, a spouse, siblings, or dear friends, it may be very painful to move on. Even in a long fulfilling life, there is never enough time during our lives to spend with our loved ones. There is a reason people use the phrase "life is short ". What if at the point of death, there are people who still need you. Who will take care of them? It can be difficult for us to accept that our loved ones have their spiritual evolution to go through as well and you leaving them is part of the path they are on. Spirits who feel guilty for dying or feel that they would be abandoning them if they crossed over, are keeping themselves bound to the physical plane. When this happens, they may become a spiritual protector and continue to watch over their loved ones for many years, if not the entire lifetime of the person involved.

It may be comforting to the spirit as well as the living person if the spirit is around to guard and protect the loved one. I, personally, do not feel that every time a spirit is attached to the physical plane it is a bad thing. There are things in the Universe that we do not understand. There may be karmic reasons that a spirit remains close to loved ones after death. In my book, *Deeper Into the Underworld: Death, Ancestors, and Magical Rites,* I talk about how we ask our ancestors to help us in healing, magick, and protection. Working with our ancestors is sacred, and it is something we should all incorporate in our spirituality. However, when we work with our ancestors it is usually ancestors who have been dead for at least a year. Also, when creating an ancestral shrine, we speak with the ancestors we wish to honor and agree to work with each other. When a spirit becomes a guardian or protector spirit, the living person must decide if that is something they would like or not. They also have to use their best judgement and decide if working with that spirit is for the best for everyone involved.

Sometimes, a spirit who has acted as a guardian or protector for someone may eventually become hostile and aggressive. They may act against the wishes of the living and do things they feel is for the best but in actuality is causing annoyance or harm. This can sometimes happen when the guardian dead has forgotten their purpose of remaining as a protector and begins to direct the life of the loved one.

Fear of Otherside

I'm not going. No. I'm fine exactly where I am. This is fine. I'm happy here. It doesn't matter. I'm fine. You don't know what's on the other side. You say you know, but do you really know? My whole life people told me about Hell and the devil and torment. I never believed any of it. I didn't think any of it was real. I just didn't believe in any of it. How could there be a cruel god that lets people burn in hell? I thought it was all bullshit. So, fuck the Bible. Fuck religion. And fuck sins and shit. I decided to live my life like I wanted. I fucked who I wanted. I did drugs if I wanted; and I stole if I wanted. Fuck it. No, I never hurt anyone. Not really. I wanted to have fun and if I hurt someone's feelings – oh, well! Then I died. I fucking died. I didn't just black out into nothing. I'm a goddamn spirit! Then I saw someone came to me and was like "Follow me!" and I was like, "Hell, no!" I'm not about to follow someone back to hell. I'm not going! I'm fine exactly where I am.

The spirit world can be confusing to people who were taught a religious background of heaven and hell, or reward and punishment. They may have been taught throughout life that if you do not obey the commands of their religious teachings then you will go to an unpleasant place. Upon death, the spirit may be too frightened to follow their ancestors to the afterlife. What they often do not realize is that no one is spiritually "perfect", and we have made many mistakes during our journey of life. I often teach my students who are learning energy healing from me that we do not know all the things that someone has gone through as they walked upon their own spiritual journey. Even if we know of their hardships, we will never truly understand their upbringing, hopes, fears, and other influences and circumstances that caused them to make the decisions that they did at the time. I have come to realize that people are doing the best they can with the situation at the time. It is not for us to judge people upon death, but rather to help upon their path of spiritual healing.

The fear of the Otherside can be very great and the spirit may refuse to cross over. They may believe that they will be punished for some perceived wrongdoing or simply for not believing in the teachings of the religion they were born into. Even though their ancestors can try to show them that no harm will come to them, their fear of the unknown is overpowering to them and they would rather stay on the physical plane rather than have their worst fears realized.

Anger and Resentment

I died in this apartment. Right there in the bedroom. I wanted to die at home. The hospitals didn't want us anyway. They called it the "gay disease." It was AIDS. They were afraid of us, the doctors and the nurses. Not all were bad, but they didn't want us there. I had my friend bring me back home. To die in a place that was familiar. I could barely walk up the stairs back here, but I did it. The righteous bastards hated us. They were glad we were dying. I had so many friends die because of this disease. Those bastards said God was punishing us for being perverts. Fuck them! I was having the time of my life. I finally lived in a big city and had gay friends. This is where I wanted to be. Away from my family who would never accept me. I was finally living my life the way I wanted. I was happy. I was so happy. Then people started getting sick. They started dying. It was just so fucking unfair. What kind of god would do that to people who just wanted to be happy and live their lives the way they wanted to? No, I'm not going. This is where I lived. This is where I was happy, and this is where I will stay.

Anger and resentment are powerful emotions. It can give some spirits energetic strength, direction, and purpose. Everyone has the right to their feelings of anger. Anger is an emotion that helps us understand the situation that happened which violated our boundaries. Anger is not a bad emotion. Anger can help us stand up for ourselves and speak our minds. It helps us gather our strength to fight against that which harmed us. For a spirit of the dead, if the anger is very great it can bind them to the physical plane. They may not even be aware that they are here on this earth because of their anger.

Spirits of the dead who stay behind because they are angry feel justified in their actions. Something during their lives, or deaths, went wrong for them and they will not cross over. There are many reasons a spirit may have anger and resentment. For some, they may stay out of retribution for those who did them wrong. I have seen instances where a spirit will not cross over because they feel that their lives were cut short. It is very difficult for some people who have died to understand and accept that there is a greater spiritual reason for their deaths. Most of us understand that there is a greater spiritual reason for many matters. But when something bad happens to us, it is really hard for us to see the spiritual reason. At death, it may be even more unclear for some people. Why does their life have to be cut short when a criminal gets to live? With this resentment spirits may often stay in the home they once lived in.

Bound by Grief

I took a handful of pills. I was ready to go. I was not afraid of death. I don't believe in hell, so I wasn't too worried about that. I guess you could say I believe in a higher power but not God. Well, not like how people talk about God. I wanted my life on Earth to end. I was tired of always feeling depressed. Half the time I didn't feel anything at all. That was the weirdest part of it. I wasn't upset when I took those pills. I was just tired. I opened my eyes and I knew something had changed. I was not in my body. Sort of like just there. Not floating really, but not standing up. I saw my grandparents who had died some years back and an aunt, I think. I didn't recognize her, but I knew she was family. I wanted to go with them. Any place would be better than here. But when I tried to go through the opening I couldn't pass through. Damn it! Why couldn't I pass through? I have seen enough ghost shows to know that when the door opens you go through and it's a much better place. I looked back at my body and there he was crying. Saying "No, don't go! I won't let you go!" But I wanted to go. He was crying so much that he was holding me back. Now, I'm here. I'm here waiting until he stops crying.

Everyone experiences grief in different ways. There is no right or wrong way to go through the process of grief. I have seen a few instances when someone had died suddenly, and their loved ones are so grief stricken that they are psychically binding the spirit to the physical plane. Our energetic attachment to a loved one can be quite strong. They can feel this connection from far away and even through space and time. This same strong connection can act as energetic shackles that keep the spirit from crossing over to the realm of the ancestors. The survivors of sudden and tragic deaths do not mean to keep the spirit here. They may not even realize how strong their psychic abilities are. They cannot help but want their loved one back and to be alive and healthy. They want things to be like they were.

In magick, we are always saying that our minds have much psychic power. We can heal the sick and change the world. If we add our psychic ability to the strong emotional grief that overwhelms us, we can unleash a great amount of magical and psychic power that we have kept deep inside our subconscious. The same psychic power that can control and bind spirit for magick, can inadvertently bind the spirit of our loved ones to the physical plane. If this happens, we have two people to heal. We will have to help heal the living loved one who is overcome with grief. My advice with this situation is to try to convince the living person to receive the healing that they need. If they do not, you can send healing energy to their helper spirits and guides so they can help the person the best way they can. You can also magically cut the energetic chords that are binding the spirit to the physical plane. This will allow the spirit to be free to journey to the Land of the Ancestors. Once again, we should not judge the living person. Grief is a powerful thing and we will never truly know what the person is going through because we will never be them. Compassion and an open heart are the true marks of a healer.

Chapter 8

Guiding the Spirit

There are many reasons why a spirit may be earthbound and either cannot or has chosen not to travel to the realm of the ancestors. As psychopomps we are healers and we must maintain as much compassion as we can for each spirit of the dead with whom we come into contact. Each person has their own path and journey they must follow. Even if we know what happened during someone's life and the circumstances of their death, it does not mean we truly understand what the person has gone through. We can only imagine what their life must have been like through our own limited perspective. As a healer, I have come to understand that people try to make the best decisions they can by using both their strengths and coping mechanisms obtained during traumatic experiences in their life. What this means is, that people can handle certain things with ease, while others are doing the best they can based on the experiences they had in life. Our job as a guide for the spirit is not to judge them but rather help them find healing by journeying to the world of the ancestors.

I have found that it is easier to escort some spirits to the afterlife, while others take a little bit more convincing and, of course, healing. Many spirits do not realize that they are dead, and it is up to us to explain to them that their time upon the physical plane has come to an end and it is time for them to move on. Other spirits may cling to unfinished business, addictive behaviors, seek justice, or attach themselves to a living person for a variety of reasons. These spirits are more difficult to convince to let go of their energetic attachments to the physical plane. It is our duty to help them understand that by remaining on the earth plane they are not only inhibiting their healing and spiritual growth, but they are also causing disharmony with the living.

The Spirits that Come to You

As you become more experienced and proficient in escorting the spirits to the afterlife, there will be times that the spirits will come to you for help. In my experience, I have found that most of the time I am asked to help a spirit cross over either by a living person or by one of my spirit guides. As your skills as a psychopomp become stronger, your aura and energy bodies will begin to vibrate on a higher octave. Anytime you are doing any type of spiritual work or working with healing energy, your energies become more refined and are balanced. Think of the times that you participated in a good ceremony or meditation and you felt yourself become light, happy, and connected to the Universe. You were able to feel your energies vibrate higher. To the spirits, we essentially become the equivalent of a spiritual lighthouse. Spirits who are in need of your assistance are able to detect your energies though both space and time.

Sometimes, earthbound spirits may appear in your home or ritual space out of the blue. When this first happened to me, it was very disturbing. I have been sitting in my living room or having dinner with friends and all of a sudden, a spirit simply appeared before me needing some kind of help. Most of the time they were not even conscious of the fact that they came to me because they needed help. Perhaps a spirit guide or some energy guided them to me. Spirits will also come to you when you are in meditation, journeying, performing ritual, or even in the dream time. In his book *Deathwalkers: Shamanic Psychopomps, Earthbound Ghosts, and Helping Spirits in the Afterlife Realm*, David Kowalewski, PhD says:

"Sometimes psychopomps become magnets for discarnate souls needing help, and so do not select their cases but their cases select them. The ghosts may show up during dreams, since both the soul's earthbound state, and the shaman's dream state, lie at the boundary between ordinary and non-ordinary realities, thereby facilitating communication."

Finding Spirits Who Need Your Help

When you begin your practice as a psychopomp it is relatively simple to find spirits of the dead who need your help crossing over to the other side. Death is all around us and many people die each and every day. We cannot avoid death even if we would like to. I think it is important to refine your craft as a guide and healer of the dead. Especially while we are learning, it is imperative to call upon your Psychopomp Teacher and ask them to take you to a spirit who may need your help. They can take you on a spirit journey to the person in need. They will then be able to guide you as you help them release earthly attachments, energetically heal, and guide them to the afterlife. Make sure that you are following the instructions of your teacher as closely as you can.

Many witches and Spirit Walkers who have psychopomp training do not seek out spirits who need help, but rather wait until their services are called upon. There are many reasons why someone might want to work in this way. They may have busy schedules with daily work, teaching, and other obligations that do not allow them to go looking for lost spirits. Also, psychopomp work may be one out of many healing modalities that they offer, and they may have made the decision to only do this work when specifically asked. Each healer makes their own path and their own choices and however they chose to walk their path of healing is wonderful for them.

Preparation for the Journey

Any time we do any kind of ecstatic witchcraft or Spirit Walking we have to prepare for the journey to the best of our abilities.

We all have busy lives and our daily routines can be dizzying at times leaving us feeling drained. Before we begin to work with the spirit of the dead, it is important that we take care of ourselves. We must make sure that our physical health is at the best it can be. As magical practitioners we should strive to be as healthy as we can . That does not mean that everyone has to be an athlete and become vegan. That is not the case at all. I do think it is important to make as many healthy life choices as you can. In our modern world that can be difficult at times. Try to be as healthy as you can and that will be fine. We also need to make sure we are getting plenty of rest. If we perform spirit work while we are mentally and physically drained that can open us to a few problems. First and foremost, it is difficult to maintain a connection with the spirits if we are exhausted and run down. Our energies will be weak and open us up to negative energies and spirit attachments. We have to make sure we are as alert as we can be. The healthier we are the more of a connection we will have to the energies of the earth and maintain a strong connection to the physical plane.

Each of us must make our own life choices, but when it comes to spirit work, I do not think any hallucinatory drugs, such as witches' ointments, ayahuasca, or peyote, are a good idea while working with the dead. One reason is that drugs such as these may impair your psychic abilities and interfere with spirit communication. Another reason is that these drugs may cause you to manifest illusionary things that are from your own mind. This can be confusing because it will be difficult to distinguish spiritual phenomenon from things in your subconscious mind. Also, hallucinatory drugs may interfere with cognitive thinking and you may have a hard time communicating with the spirit. On a personal level, I think substances like peyote, ayahuasca, and witch's ointment have spiritual value when done under the guide of a spiritual leader in ceremonial use. When it comes to working with the spirits of the dead, I feel it is better to be free of any intoxicants that may impair your spiritual work.

Before you do any psychopomp work, make sure that your ritual space is energetically clean and protected. If you are journeying to work with a spirit you can place basic wards around your working space and that will do the trick because you are not inviting energies to your space, you are journeying to them. If you are conjuring the spirit to your ritual space, make sure that you have strong protective wards in place. It does not happen very often, but there are times that when you are summoning a spirit of the dead into your ritual space it creates a portal from the spirit world. This can allow trickster and dark spirits to come through. Your protective wards will prevent this from happening. I, personally, prefer to wear a protective charm, necklace, or magical ring when I do any kind of spirit work. This prevents spirits from trying to influence my energies or, even worse, trying to possess my body. Again, this is rare, but if you feel protected then you will have more confidence in your work, especially in the beginning.

Psychopomp Ritual Outline

Whenever I am performing a ritual or ceremony, I prefer to keep a ritual outline handy. Even the most experienced ritualist can jumble the sequence of the ritual so for that reason I usually keep a small piece of paper handy with my outline. There are no set words or lines. Everything you say to the spirits are to be said from a place of compassion and healing so, as long as the words come from your heart, you will be fine. Each section of the outline will be explained in further detail.

Calling Upon Your Psychopomp Teacher and Guides - Before you begin any kind of psychopomp work you will need to call upon your gods, goddesses, ancestors, and Psychopomp Teacher. Of all the steps in spirit work, this is the most important. Remember, the spirits can see more energy than you will be able to see. They also have a different perspective on the energy world as well as the flow of time. Not everyone works with gods during psychopomp work, but many of us do. If you are working with deities who open the way between worlds, such as Hekate, Mercury, or Eshu, it is important that you call upon them and ask them to open the veil between the worlds for you. Witches have the power to open the veil between the worlds ourselves, but when we call upon the powers of a deity, they can open the portals in a very powerful way. They can also give you an insight on any dangers that may occur in doing so. If any of these liminal gods are also your Psychopomp Teacher, then all the better! Working with the gods and goddesses of the Underworld also has a great advantage. The gods who guard and protect the ancestors are very powerful and sometimes they will not allow you to pass into the ancestral realm unless you have their permission. Even if you do not honor the gods of the Underworld, it will be beneficial to have a working relationship with them.

As with other parts of your psychopomp work, you will call upon your Psychopomp Teacher. Until you are very experienced with guiding the spirits to the Land of the Ancestors you will call upon your Psychopomp Teacher every single time for guidance and advice with your work. Your teacher will be able to guide you through the process of guiding the dead to the Land of the Ancestors. They will be able to help you troubleshoot situations that may come up. There may be some situations that happen with spirits that you did not count on. Many of the situations that occur will be relatively easy to navigate through, but in the event, something comes up that you did not expect, the Psychopomp Teacher will be able to guide through difficult situations.

Your ancestors are also another important spiritual guide that you will have for your psychopomp work. Once your ancestors begin working with you magically, they will be able to assist you in spirit work a great deal. As we have said before, they have the ability to see energies we cannot see. They have the ability to tell you what is happening with the spirit of the dead and their energies. Once your ancestors are proficient in reading energies, they will be able to access memories, thoughts, and feelings from the spirit you may not have access too. The most important reason that you should call upon your ancestors with psychopomp work is because they can help you call upon the spirit's ancestors from the afterlife. This is probably the most important part of psychopomp work. The spirit will be very reluctant to cross over unless they can be reassured by a family member in spirit. I have found that it is crucial to have your ancestors as guides and spirit healers.

Psychic History - Once you have called your gods, ancestors, and Psychopomp Teacher, it is time to do the actual work of the psychopomp. Before you summon the spirit of the dead, it is very important that you get as much information as possible. If at all possible, you will need to go to the location of the person's death and find out everything you can on the person themselves as well as the circumstances of their death. The location of a death will contain the psychic echo of the events that lead to the person's death. It does not matter how long ago the death occurred. You will still be able to tap into the energies of the past. We will need to psychically tap into those energies so that we will have a better understanding of what happened. We will also get the information the best we can from the spirit themselves.

So why do we need to also tap into the environment in which the death occurred? We do this to get a more objective point of view of the circumstances surrounding the person's death. Have you ever been witness to two people who were involved in an accident of some sort, such as a car wreck? Both people will have a different view on what happened to cause the accident. It does not mean that one of the people telling the story is wrong, it means that each of us experiences events through our own lens of perception. Being human, we cannot possibly see things from all angles with detailed perception. That is just how we are made. We see things through our own emotions and mental state as well as the limited point of view that we have. So, when we speak to the spirit who died, they cannot be objective when it comes to their own death. We cannot possibly expect them to be objective. How could they? By getting more psychic information we will be able to see the whole story as it stands and be better prepared to help the spirit cross over to the realm of the ancestors.

We have all walked into a room and felt a weird vibe. With a little bit of psychic focus, we could feel what just transpired just hours or moments ago. The air seems thick with energy waiting to tell you a story. Energy can stay contained in a room for a very long time. An energetically charged room is actually quite common. This is one of the purposes of smudging with sage or mugwort. The smudge energetically cleans the room we are in. When someone dies, especially from a death that is violent, tragic, or unexpected, there is a psychic echo that is imprinted in the room or even in an outside area. The energetic process of dying creates a portal between the worlds. Add the emotional distress of violence, sadness, or rage and the echo can be felt for years after the time of death took place. People with psychic senses can pick up on these energies very easily.

Sensing the events that took place in a room of a home or outside is not as hard as it may sound. Essentially it is a similar technique to scrying. Instead of gazing into black bowl or magick mirror, you will be looking "into" the space where the death occurred.

1. Stand in the spot where you sense that the energies of the death are strongest.

2. Connect with your gods, guides, and Psychopomp Teacher. Be open to any suggestions they may have about this process.

3. Open your heart chakra and your third eye chakra.

4. You may close your eyes or keep them open. Whichever way is easier for you to see the energies.

5. Visualize your Sphere of Sensation expanding to the whole area you are in. Be open to any thoughts, feelings, sounds, or sights you may see.

6. While you are connecting to the energies in the space, visualize that your consciousness, or your center, is going back in the past, back to where the death occurred. You may ask your Psychopomp Teacher to help your consciousness go back (it may help to visualize your consciousness or your "center" as a sphere of white light). Know that you have the ability to see the events of the past.

7. You can either speak aloud or in your mind. Ask what happened here. Ask the energies how the person died. Take some nice deep breaths and continue to connect with the energies. Watch how the events unfold. Remember that you are seeing a psychic recording of the death. We cannot intervene in any way.

8. Once you are finished, thank the energies and the spirits.

9. You may wish to write down what you observed so that you will be prepared when you speak to the spirit.

If you are doing this work and you are unable to physically walk into the place where the death occurred, you can journey in spirit to the place and perform the same techniques. Physically being present is always better, but journeying there will do as well.

Meeting the Spirit - When we first meet the spirit who is earthbound, there are a few things you need to keep in mind.

Always approach the spirit with kindness, compassion, and a healer's mindset. Having a healer's mindset means that our intent is to help the spirit heal and to do no harm. Psychopomp work is definitely a healing modality. By guiding the dead to the afterlife, you are facilitating a healing experience for the spirit. This is why I said at the beginning of this book that by doing this work you are a healer. What sets a healer apart from other forms of medical or energy work is that you must learn to have compassion for every single spirit of the dead that you work with. You may discover that many of the spirits you are asked to work with were not very good people in life. You may come to find that many of them hurt people for profit or simply out of anger and confusion. It is not for us to judge the dead, but to help them begin their steps in their own healing process. Once you help a spirit find their way to the afterlife, their personal guides and ancestors will start their healing journey. You may also meet spirits who are addicts, drunk drivers, and violent people. Again, we have to have compassion for them. As healers, our job is to help bring spirits into balance the best we can. We also may not have all the information that caused the spirit to do what they did while they were alive. Again, it is not for us to pass judgement. Only to help them cross over so they can get the healing that they need.

It is very common that the spirit may not know that they are dead. We do not want to abruptly tell a spirit they are dead because this will only cause more confusion. This is another reason we want to approach all spirits of the dead with compassion. Imagine being at work one day and some stranger comes up to you and says, "By the way, you're dead!" Not only will you think they have lost their mind, you will also think they are being rude and aggressive. This does not foster trust between you and the spirit. It may sound strange that a spirit might not know they are dead. When a person has a disease or is hospitalized, they have time to mentally and emotionally prepare themselves for death. Hopefully, they come to accept their death and that they will soon join their ancestors, gods, and spirits. When someone dies abruptly, they may be in shock and in great denial. Have you ever had the experience of being in shock because of some tragic event? Your emotions are all over the place and your mind may have a hard time processing the event that happened. Upon death, their astral and spirit bodies are released from their physical body. They will still feel the same as they did when they were alive. From their point of view, they may still feel just as alive as they ever did. They may feel pleasure and pain and have the same cognitive functions. For those who have a deep rooted Christian religious upbringing, they may have learned that at the moment of death they will be taken to heaven or hell. Since neither of those things have happened, they may think that they cannot possibly be dead. As best we can, we have to explain to the person that they have died. If you keep kindness, compassion, and a healer's mindset, the person should be more receptive to hearing and understanding that they are dead.

When we first meet the person, we must introduce ourselves just as we would any living person. Never think of the spirit as less than a living person. If your ancestors, gods, guides, and Psychopomp Teacher are visible to the spirit make sure you introduce them to the person as well. Introductions are important because it is the first step in building trust between you and the spirit. You are beginning a relationship, even if it is only a healer-client relationship. Be mindful of your tone of voice and your own energies. If you are upset, angry, or sick, this is not the time to do psychopomp work. Spirits of the dead are more perceptive than you might think. They can often tell when something is wrong with you. When we are meeting the spirit of the dead be prepared for anything to happen. Prepare yourself for the worst while hoping for the best possible outcome.

Listening to their Story - Every one of us has a story. Our stories are unique to us and they give others a glimpse into who we are and the characteristics that we possess. Some stories are triumphant with many successes, while other stories are filled with sorrow. We all have different stories that paint the canvas of our lives. Without stories we would have an uneventful and stagnant life with very little spiritual growth. Listening to the story of the person is where the healing process really begins. I personally feel that the stories that the spirit tells are the most important part of the process when it comes to guiding the spirit back home. We must be able to listen and understand the events and circumstances that led the person to where they are now. There have been many times in my younger years that I assumed I knew how a person came to be where they are. I wrongly assumed what happened to them without trying to understand the situation from their point of view. In almost every case, once I heard the actual story of the person, I realized that I was wrong and that their path was unique to them and they were taking their journey the best that they could.

The person's story is what will help us determine what caused them to become earthbound. Again, I want to reiterate that we need to approach the person's tale with a sense of kindness, compassion, and a healer's mindset. When listening to the person's story we need to make sure we are engaging in *active listening*. Active listening is where we are totally focused on what is being said without agenda or simply waiting until it is our turn to speak. We need to be completely present and supportive when listening to the person's story. Try your best not to judge their decisions that they made in life. Remember, everyone usually tries to make the best decision they can with the circumstances that they have at the time based on their upbringing and environment. What works for us may not work for someone else. Remember compassion.

At times, the spirits of the dead can become stuck in their

own drama. They may replay what has happened to them over and over again. We have all heard people repeat the same story to us over and over in the same conversation. They are more or less stuck in a sort of loop of their own story and dilemma. By remaining in the story loop their energies cannot get beyond the feelings and frustrations of the story that have found themselves trapped in. Energetically, by remembering the story over and over again, they are binding themselves to the story and the feelings therein. If we can get them to tell us their story, this will allow us the opportunity to help them release themselves from the negative energies of their tale.

Calling their Ancestors - Just as you called upon your ancestors, gods, guides, and Psychopomp Teacher, you will need to call upon the spirit's ancestors as well. There is no stronger spiritual link than the one we have with our ancestors. Yes, the gods are powerful, but they are connected to the greater Universe and the welfare of all involved. The ancestors are our family and they are connected through the energetic bonds of our bloodlines. Through their love and compassion for the spirit, you will have a greater chance in bringing them home to be with their ancestors. The spirit that you are working with may be upset, angry, or confused and it is important that the family is involved in both the healing process as well as guiding them to the afterlife. To the spirit you are helping, you are a stranger. They do not know you and they do not truly know what your intentions are. Having people who are familiar to them will help them to feel more comfortable with the healing process.

The best and easiest way I have found to call upon the person's ancestors is by asking your ancestors to bring them from the Land of the Ancestors. Your ancestors have the ability to quickly find the spirit's ancestors and ask them to help in escorting them back with them. You may be asking yourself, "How are they able to do that?" The ancestors are not bound by space and time as we are here in the physical plane. They have the ability to read the spirit's energetic signature of their bloodline. They can then search the spirit world and ask their ancestors to help you with your work. Personally, I have never had someone's ancestors not come. Even if there are grievances from the past, the ancestors are able to put their differences aside in order to help their loved ones cross over to the other side. In my experience, I have found that the person's ancestors can appear by coming through a portal from the ancestral realm or simply appear before you. When they come to you, remember to greet them and thank them for helping in the healing session.

Energy Healing - Before we can help the spirit transition to the afterlife, we have to make sure that the person is in a place of balance the best we can. Thoughts and emotions cause damage and imbalances to someone's spirit. When the person is under great stress or duress the person's energies become chaotic or very weak and this will inhibit them from being able to transition to the realm of the ancestors. We have all heard the term "like attracts like". What this means is that when thoughts and emotions affect someone's energy body and spirit in a negative way, they will attract negative energies and spirits. Also, negative thought patterns will cause the spirit to vibrate on a lower level and many not allow them to travel to their ancestral home in the afterlife. This can happen when someone dies of violence, tragedy, addiction, or great sorrow. It is vital that we perform energy healing to the spirit so they can transition in a balanced way.

With the help of your spirit guides and Psychopomp Teacher, use your psychic vision and scan the spirit for spirit attachments, spirit intrusions, and tendrils of energy that may be binding the spirit to the physical plane. You can use a crystal or consecrated dagger or blade to cut away these things. Simply visualize the attachment or tendrils and cut them away from the spirit. Visualize a portal opening up in the ground and visualize these things being sent into the Abyss so they can be properly taken care of by the entities therein.

The next thing you will need to do is send healing energy to the person so their energies can be restored and balanced. If you know reiki, you may use the reiki symbols and energies. If you do not have training in energy work, you can still be able to perform healing energy work. It is easier than you may think.

1. Bring your consciousness to the deep Universe in the Upperworld.
2. Open your heart chakra and bring to mind thoughts of love, healing, and balance .
3. Know that the Universe is filled with the healing energies of creation and the entire matrix of the Universe is that of growth and healing.
4. Take a deep breath in and visualize a beam of white light entering your crown chakra and moving into your heart chakra. As you exhale, visualize this Universal healing energy moving through your arms and out of your hands sending a beam of healing energy to the spirit.
5. Visualize the person receiving this beautiful Universal healing energy. See the energy restoring the spirit and bringing them into a place of balance. While you are sending energy to the spirit, also visualize the person's ancestors, your guides, and your Psychopomp Teacher sending them healing energy as well.
6. Give thanks to the Universe for sending you the healing energy.

By sending healing energy to the spirit you are helping them adjust their energies so that they will be mentally, emotionally, and energetically in a better place to understand why they must transition to the afterlife. Think of it this way, when you are sick with the flu you are far less likely to hear someone's explanation of why you should do something. Once you are feeling better and balanced you are in a better place to understand someone's point of view.

Spiritual Counseling - Now that you and your guides have sent healing energy to the spirit, they will be in a better state of being to understand why they should transition to the afterlife. In my healing practice, I try to understand that a person's journey is complicated and I could never truly understand what they have gone through. The person is doing the best they can with the circumstances and upbringing they received. It is also important to keep in mind that everyone processes information and experiences differently and we can never truly know someone's thought process. It is at this stage that we try to explain to the spirit why they should join their ancestors to the best of our ability. Everyone has the ability of free will and the choice to cross over is ultimately that of the spirit. It is up to us to try and help them understand it is in their best interest to travel into the afterlife.

After listening to the person's story, I do my best to understand why the person could not or chose not to go through the portal with their ancestors. If they had fear, I try to empathize with their fear. If they had unfinished business, then I try to help them let go of that need to finish their business or perhaps help finish it if it is in my ability and will to do so. For example, if a person needs to know what became of their child, if I can do the research and find out for them, I am happy to do so. It does not take too long in our digital age. However, if their unfinished business is more complicated and time consuming, for example, wanting to see their family business grow into fruition, then I have to explain to them to trust those who are running the business now and they are free to enjoy their afterlife. Sometimes, the spirit is seeking justice for a wrong done to them. I can understand them wanting to wait for justice. I think it is natural to do so. Again, we have to help the person understand that other people are taking care of the crime and they are free to have peace. Another complicated situation is one where the spirit is an addict. Many times, addicted spirits can become psychic vampires and drain energy from living addicts or siphon energy from places that house addicts. They rarely take energy from non-addicts; they are looking for an energetic fix and living addicts are the best way to do that. In my experience, I have helped them heal with energy healing and helped them understand that their addiction will be addressed and healed with healing spirits in the afterlife. Their days of suffering and wanting will be over when they get the help they need in the spirit world.

The spirits who do not know that they have died are more challenging for me. Many spirits who do not crossover made a choice for some reason not to cross the portal to the ancestors, but the ones who do not understand they are dead are confused and bewildered to their current circumstance. The energy world can be shaped by our thoughts and emotions. As I have said before, spirits are more connected to the energy world at the point of death. Their thoughts and emotions will shape their version of reality, or rather the energy is shaped by what they *think* is real. In other words, sometimes the person goes on living their day to day life because they do not know not to. Take a moment and imagine a life where you lived alone and did not communicate to many people. Perhaps you worked alone and did not venture out of your home very often. If you suddenly died, you may continue to perform your daily routine. With these spirits, you can perhaps show them a current newspaper or perhaps show them their own gravestone. You can even show them the current residents in their home. You do this by taking them on a spirit journey to these locations. It is very important to be gentle and kind. They may be very upset and you do not want them to have a mental breakdown, but allow them the space to have their emotions about suddenly realizing they are dead. Remember the first rule of psychopomp work is to have the mindset of a healer, kindness, and compassion.

Make sure you are learning from your Psychopomp Teacher about how to counsel the people who have not crossed over. The important thing to remember in this part of the work is that we have to help them understand that by staying on the earth plane they are keeping themselves from healing and happiness. The Land of the Ancestors contains spiritual healers and guides who can help them understand the transition process and their greater connection to the Universe. I have seen some psychopomps explain to spirits that the physical plane is not meant for them and they should move to the realm of the ancestors even if they do not want to because they do not belong here. That may be true, but that is not showing compassion and really *hearing* the person. Yes, they are a spirit, but they are still a person. When a person sees that we are trying to help them because we want to help them heal, they will be able to sense that energy and may be more open to listening to what we have to say. Every day I see people asking, "what does it all mean?" People feel more assured when they understand there is a greater spiritual purpose for everything. When we are spiritually advising spirits, look to your gods, ancestors, and Psychopomp Teacher for help in what to say and how to say it. Every single person has a unique story and every situation is going to be different. Listen to them, send healing energy to them, and to the best of your ability help them understand that letting go of the attachments of Earth is an act of strength and spiritual evolution.

Journeying to the Land of the Ancestors - Once a spirit has decided to release the energetic bonds tying them to the physical plane, they are ready to transition to the afterlife. One of the wonderful things about psychopomp work is that no one is left alone. There is a spiritual community that is involved in this beautiful process. The spirits understand that it can be very frightening and sometimes overwhelming to journey from this world to the world of the ancestors. Everything changes. From this point forward there will be many things that the person will experience that they most likely never imagined. All good things. All things that help the person heal, rejuvenate, and spiritually evolve. Even though wonderful things will happen in the afterlife, it can still be very overwhelming. This is why we guide the spirit with the help of their ancestors and other spirits. This transition is an act of healing and compassion.

The person's ancestors play a very important role in guiding them to the ancestral realm. Even if they are ancestors from a distant part of their bloodline, they will help the person feel at ease and more at home. There will be an energetic bond of family that will be comforting to them. Their ancestors that come to greet the them are ones who are well versed in traveling between the worlds. They will know how to open the portal to the afterlife and how to get home. In the energetic world of the afterlife, in order to get home one must only think of the ancestors and they will be taken there in an instant. If the person worked with gods and other spiritual beings, such as ascended masters, they may also help escort the person to the Land of the Ancestors. Usually, these are beings the person honored in life. Not all gods and goddesses will help escort a person to the afterlife, but you may be surprised about who will. I have found for pagans and witches our gods are compassionate towards us even after death.

There will be times that the person feels very comfortable with their ancestors and gods and they will not require you to guide them to the afterlife. You have helped them heal and helped them take the first steps into the beginning of an incredible journey. If this is the case, then give your blessings and farewells. Thank the person's ancestors and spirits for helping in this process. At this time there is nothing more you need to do. Your healing work is done for today. I think of it as a family matter at this point. You helped bring the family together and now it is up to them to do the rest.

People can be emotionally overwhelmed or frightened so there will be instances where you will need to guide the person into the Land of the Ancestors yourself. As a healer, you may be needed to walk with the person to the ancestral realm. If you have been practicing the journeying exercises in this book, then you will have no trouble at all. There are a couple of different ways you can get to the world of the ancestors. If the person's ancestors came through a portal that is still open they can simply go back through that portal. If it has closed, then you can open a new portal with a magical dagger, a wand, or just your finger. To do this, focus your heart and mind on the ancestral realm.

1. You may sit or lie down. Place yourself in a relaxed state. You can drum or play a drumming recording if you like, but music is not necessary. Visualize yourself actually getting up from your body.
2. Take a moment to get our bearings and reconnect to your Psychopomp Teacher, ancestors, and guides as well as the spirit of the dead and their ancestors.
3. Now it is time to travel to the Land of the Ancestors. Remember the feelings of the warm beautiful place and visualize the Land of the Ancestors. Deepen your psychic connection with your heart.
4. Then take the dagger, wand, or your finger and visualize create an energetic line in the air. This is essentially "cutting" an opening between this world and the world of the ancestors.
5. Then take both hands and open the line into a doorway just as you would open curtains from the center.
6. Once the portal is open, it is time for you to guide the

spirit back home. Reassure them again about how much happier they will be in this magical land.

7. Allow the person's ancestors to lead the way so they may take them to be reunited with all of their ancestors. Along with your Psychopomp Teacher, your guides and spirits, walk with the person and answer any questions they may have.

Another technique you can do is a shamanic teleportation to the ancestral realm.

1. You may sit or lie down. Place yourself in a relaxed state. You can drum or play a drumming recording if you like, but music is not necessary. Visualize yourself astrally getting up from your body.
2. Remember what it feels like from your journeys there. Feel the warmth, love, and healing energies of this wonderful place.
3. Stand next to the person you are guiding and their ancestors. Visualize a large beam of white light at your feet.
4. See the beam of white light spiral around you, the person you are guiding, and all the spirits you have called into the space. Visualize the spiral of white light encasing you and the spirits in a cocoon of white energy.
5. As the white light spirals around, know that his energy is teleporting you to the Land of the Ancestors.

Once you and the spirits have arrived at the ancestral world, you should be greeted by the person's ancestors as well as healing spirits and guides. The spirits are well aware that you are coming. They may even have intervened on the person's behalf and asked you to help psychopomp the person home. In the very unlikely event that the person's ancestors do not appear upon your arrival, call out to the ancestors with your mind and your heart telling them their family member has come home. Even if their immediate family does not appear, someone in their family line should come and help the person in their next steps.

Returning Home - It is very heartwarming to see someone reunited with their ancestors and know that they will get the healing that they need. For myself, this is the best part of the whole psychopomp process. Sometimes after years of being on the physical plane in spirit, someone is finally receiving the help that they need. It is time for you to return home. All you have to do is imagine yourself back in your ritual space and you will be there at the speed of thought. Make sure that you cut any energetic chords that you may have acquired during the psychopomp process.

Clearing the Space - Before ending the ceremony, make sure you clear your space of any excess energy, spiritual debris, or negative influences. When a spirit tells you their story it can be quite traumatic, and their emotions may fill your ritual space with negative energy. Be sure to cleanse your space. You may use a fumigation with sage, frankincense, mugwort, or copal. You can also use reiki symbols or runes to place in the four corners of your space. Or you can use any energy banishing techniques you like.

Offerings and Thanks - The very last thing you will need to do to end your ceremony is to give your ancestors, guides, gods, and Psychopomp Teacher thanks and offerings. We always give offerings when the spirits help us. Offerings can include water, food, wine, candles, incense, and prayers.

Self-Care

It is very important to take care of yourself after working with the spirits of the dead in any capacity. On an emotional level, the spirits will tell you their stories and some of them are very hard to hear. They will tell us of their heartaches, tragedies, and disappointments. When you are acting as a healer and guide you are there for them. You are there to support them and their needs. This is a lot easier said than done. When we are helping others, we cannot help but to become invested in the person, even if it is just a little bit. We want them to heal and get better. We want them to be happy. As we know, life does not always work out the way we want it to. Things happen out of our control that causes pain and suffering. Things also happen that we caused ourselves. People make mistakes and poor decisions at times. This does not make us bad people. It makes us human. When we are listening to the stories of the spirits, we have maintained the healer's mind. We have to push our own feelings aside so that we can be supportive for the person who needs our help. Anytime you work with the spirits and journey to the three worlds it will be energetically and physically draining. Even though we have our spiritual guides, gods, and ancestors are helping us with the magick it will drain some of our energies.

There are many things we can do for self-care. Every day we need to make sure that we are in the best physical, mental, emotional, and energetic health possible. Having psychic and magical power does not mean we should neglect our own wellbeing. This does not mean you need to be in "perfect" health. But we do need to take care of ourselves to the best of our ability. Make sure you get plenty of exercise and the proper nutrition for YOU. No, you do not need to be a vegetarian or vegan to be a powerful witch or healer. For some, veganism helps with this. For others it does not. Do what works for you. Proper sleep is needed as well. Our bodies need to heal and regenerate for proper function. Also, lack of sleep can make some people vulnerable to some energies. I also think it's important to be spiritually connected to the Universe. Honor your gods and spirits and keep the energetic connection as strong as possible. The stronger the connection between you and your spirits the more likely they will be able to help you in this work.

Self-care immediately after psychopomp work is important. If you need to ground the energies, then do so. Even advanced witches can be the worst ones when it comes to grounding. We often forget to do our basic psychic work when performing rituals. When the ritual is over, make sure you disconnect from the energies in some way. Have food and drinks with your circle or your friends. It may sound silly, but turn on the television, listen to music, or read a book. Anything that you enjoy that will disconnect your mind from magick is important so as not to drain you any further. The most important self-care tip I have, is to listen to your body. If you are tired, then rest. If you are hungry, then eat. If you want to get out of the house and go dancing, then go dancing. Whatever you need for you to recharge then do so.

Group Psychopomp Ritual

Performing a psychopomp ritual in a group setting can be very rewarding and very powerful. If you belong to a group or coven, your circle can easily help the spirits cross over to the afterlife. When more witches, Spirit Walkers, and healers come together the more powerful the ceremony will be. This is because when we join our energies with others the psychic energy is amplified a great deal. There are many reasons why working with a group for psychopomp work has many benefits. When you are a beginning student in the ways of the psychopomp this is a wonderful opportunity to learn from others who are more experienced. Working in a group setting builds confidence and sense of security. When I was a student, I appreciated watching the expertise of other witches and magical practitioners. I could watch others who had years of experience and see how they would handle the situations that would arise. My favorite part was watching skillful psychopomps troubleshoot problems and see how they were able to think outside the box to find a solution. Another benefit to working in a group was the added security that I felt. As a magical student I would at times wonder if I was doing techniques correctly. I would also wonder if any negative spirits would be attracted to my work and what would I do? Being in a group made me feel more at ease because I knew groups were always more powerful than one witch acting alone.

Psychopomp group ritual is a great way for everyone in your group to share the beautiful experience of guiding someone home to their ancestors. There is a special bonding that happens when people share in the healing of others. It connects you to them on a heart level as well as an energetic level. The more a group practices together, the more in sync you become with one another. As your bond grows over time, the more powerful your magick will become.

You may find yourself doing psychopomp work alone most of the time. Partly, because there are not many people who know how to do the work or not called to do the work. There is no judgement. Each of us who are magical work with the energies and spirits that are unique to us. That is one of the great things about being a witch or Spirit Walker; there is so much magick in the Universe that it calls to each of us in our own unique way. However, I found working within a circle or group can greatly expand your psychopomp abilities as well as teach you many new things. When you have the opportunity to work with others in escorting the dead it is an amazing experience.

There are different ways that you can perform a group psychopomp ritual. I prefer to have everyone in a circle and connect to each other's energies by holding hands. It is important to make sure that everyone is aware of each step of the process. This helps keep the pace of the ritual as well as keeping everyone on the same page. Each of the steps are the same as in the solitary ritual, but there are a few differences to keep in mind. First, make sure that only one person speaks at a time so as not to confuse the spirit. You can designate one person to speak or everyone can if they so choose. The other thing to take into consideration is traveling to the world of the ancestors. You have to decide if one person is going or is the entire group going. If the group is going at the same time, then it will be a good idea for everyone to practice journeying as a group beforehand. This is relatively easy to do. The important thing to remember when journeying as a group is to energetically connect with each other beforehand.

Mass Killings and Death

Here in the U.S., it seems like there are mass killings every day. There are mentally unstable people who, for some reason or another, decided to take a gun and end the life of many people. There is no rationality for this. It will never make sense why this happens. All that is left from this is pain and suffering for the living and the people who have lost their lives. War is another thing that causes multiple deaths. It seems that there is always war or military violence somewhere in the world. Many innocent lives are lost. As wars go on, there is no real winner. Every side loses and everyone is left in pain.

Guns and war are not the only things that cause mass killings and death. Many natural disasters cause multiple deaths as well. Everything from hurricanes, tornadoes, fires, earthquakes, and other disasters take countless lives every year. Disease has taken many lives as well. AIDS, cancer, COVID-19, and other diseases have taken the lives of many people. I will not try to guess what the spiritual significance is for the deaths of many.

As psychopomps, I believe it is our responsibility to help the spirits of those people who lost their lives to tragedy.

There are numerous healers from all over the world who help spiritually. There are many energy healers who send healing energy to the living so they can cope, heal, and rebuild their communities. There are healers who send healing energy to the Nature Spirits and to the land itself so it can regrow and be renewed once more. Then there are those of us who seek to heal the dead and help them find their way to the Land of the Ancestors to receive the healing that they need. The first thing I do when there is tragedy such as this is to place a white candle in my window seal. I program the candle to light the way of any spirit who needs my help transitioning back home to the ancestors. After the tragedy, many of the spirits are confused and do not understand what happened to them. They may have gotten lost trying to find their way.

Once I do that, I will journey in spirit to the sight of the tragedy and begin my healing work there. I will often find healers in spirit healing the land, the negative energies, and the spirits of those lost. Just as we clean the home before taking care of a haunting, we will clean the energy of the tragedy the best we can. I do this by tuning in to the energy and grounding it to Mother Earth to be recycled for other use. Then I will look for spirits who need help. Along with my Psychopomp Teacher, the ancestors, and my gods, I will do as much spiritual counseling as I can and guide them to the Land of the Ancestors. It is especially hard when guiding children. One of the many blessings of calling to the person's ancestors is that the spirit has a loving family to go to. No one is left behind. Nor alone. I use the same psychopomp techniques as usual to guide the spirit, but I must admit it is harder to push my emotions aside. But I am a healer for them. It is about their healing.

When it comes to guiding the spirit home to the Land of the Ancestors be patient with yourself. Continue to work with your

Psychopomp Teacher, your ancestors, and the gods and you will do fine. Remember to treat each spirit as an individual and do the best you can. Go into this work with compassion and an open heart and you will do just fine.

Chapter 9

Haunted Houses and Psychic Self-Defense

Hauntings

There are many people who believe that they have encountered a haunting. They have seen human figures out of the corner of their eye and found furniture to have been moved in their home. Some have seen the spectral shade of a person night after night in a place where something bad had happened. Others have seen the spirits of the dead in their dreams. The dreamer may see the dead trying to communicate with them. Other people may feel a human presence always watching them. They may not be able to see them, but they know that they are there. Sightings of ghosts have been found throughout the history of the human race and in many cultures. The ancient Greeks believed that if you were visited by a shade of the dead then that was a clear message that the person died tragically without proper funerary rights. In Mesopotamia, seeing the dead was an omen of sickness and disease soon to come. In Britain, there are stories of the ghost roads. It was said that witches would watch the ghostly procession of the shades carrying a coffin down the funerary road towards the cemetery. They would take a peek at who was inside for it foretold who was soon to die.

Another part of our work as a psychopomp is helping people who feel that their home is being haunted by a spirit of the dead. There are a lot of reasons they have come to believe that their home is haunted. It happens, but it is very rare, that someone actually sees the spirit with their physical eyes. It takes a spirit a lot of energy to manifest to the point where a person with very little psychic skill is able to see them. Sometimes, a person may not realize that they have some psychic ability and they may see spirits at times when no one else in the home can. I have found that people believe their home is haunted because of a few different reasons. They may feel a very strong presence. Sometimes they may have the feeling of constantly feeling watched. They may also have noticed small things, such as dishes and nick knacks being moved around. There are also audio cues such as hearing footsteps in the home or wrappings upon the walls. Some people may have nightly dreams of the same spirit trying to get into contact with them. A rarer phenomenon is the hearing of voices and whispers in the home. There are other things a spirit can do to physically manifest in the home such lights flickering on and off, cold drafts that seem to come from nowhere, and a "dark" or uneasy feeling when the spirit is present. Whenever I have been called to someone's home because of a haunting, I have found there are several different things causing a disturbance.

I have a spiritual "open door" policy. My home is warded and shielded from unwelcome spirits, but I have the shields programmed that allows spirits who need my help to come through. Also, living in an older building in Chicago, there is always a chance there could be a resident spirit in my home. I can only speak for myself, but as long as they do not bother me, they are welcome to stay. I also trust that my ancestors will not allow any spirits through who would cause a disturbance or wish me harm. For other people, having a ghost in their home can not only be disruptive, but it can be downright frightening. As witches, we welcome all sorts of spirits and ghosts parading through our home. It is just part of our cosmology and spiritual practice. To non-magical people, ghosts often remind them of their inevitable death. I think there is something built into our subconscious minds that to stay away from ghosts is a way of staying away from the energies of death and to become haunted is a great reminder that death may be lurking around the corner.

Not everyone who thinks they have a ghost are indeed experiencing a genuine haunting. The same evidence that seems to point to a spiritual intrusion can most of the time be explained by "natural causes". Many old houses have creaky floors and stairs. When storms come or air temperatures change, the wood in the house adjusts and makes a horrible creaking sound. It may sound silly, but sometimes the knocking and wrapping sounds of what we think is a ghost is nothing more than the rattling of pipes. The sudden cold draft can simply be from a wall or window that needs to be fixed. Also, for many people, the reason they see ghosts out of the corner of their eyes is because our peripheral vision is not as clear as our straight on vision and sometimes our brains are trying to make sense of the blurred images that it is perceiving.

Mental pathology can also be a reason someone believes that they are being haunted. As a psychopomp and a healer, this is perhaps the most difficult of situations when it comes to a "rational explanation" of seeing ghosts in the home. It is out of the scope of our practice to diagnose anyone with a mental pathology. However, there are some clear indications that mental issues are at play. If someone has a history of severe drug use or addiction that is a good indication that the spirits they are seeing are in their minds. Over time, certain drugs wreak havoc on the mind and some addicts may have hallucinations. There are also those people who may be hearing voices and seeing things that are not there because of mental pathology. For me, the reason this is a difficult situation is because I personally feel that when strong magical ability and psychic power are not properly trained, they can lead to psychic blockages that cause harm to a person's mental psyche. I believe this is one of the reasons people become mentally unstable. That being said, it is possible that the mentally ill are, indeed, seeing spirits and can sometimes see things in different planes of existence. This is why it is vital that the psychopomp is skilled in their psychic abilities. I have had some clients who were paranoid and believed that spirits were watching them wherever they went, but through journeys and magical work I found this was not the case. If you find yourself in this situation and you find that there are no spirits haunting someone's home, it is ok to tell them your findings and recommend another practitioner for a second opinion. It is not our place to mention mental illness, but we should not pursue it further if this is what you have come to believe. Your spiritual practice should always have integrity.

Spirits of the dead are constantly around us giving us protection, wisdom, and guidance. Part of our spiritual practice is to call upon our ancestors and other spirits of the dead. The spirits who help us in our daily lives and our spiritual path are not classified as spirits who haunt us. Non-magical people most likely will not notice if the ancestors are near or not. A true haunting is a different matter entirely. A true haunting occurs when the dead are restless, angry, lost, or confused. Many of them do not know that they are dead. Many times, when someone is experiencing symptoms of a haunting it is the spirit's way of trying to communicate with them. Some spirits may need help while others are very unhappy that the living are occupying their home. These spirits are in need of the aid of a Psychopomp. Michelle Belanger says in her book, *The Ghost Hunter's Survival Guide: Protection Techniques For Encounters With The Paranormal:*

"For many, the very fact that they still linger close to the physical world is a clear indication of emotional issues. Murder victims, suicides, victims of prolonged abuse, and individuals whose deaths were particularly traumatic often remain until they are able to reconcile themselves with the lingering issues of both their life and their death."

Psychic Echoes

A psychic echo is not the same thing as a human spirit of the dead who has taken up residence in someone's home. A psychic echo can be observed as a spirit who seems to do the same exact thing night after night around the same time. There are many stories of this nature such as a woman walking up the staircase each night to check on the children sleeping soundly in their bedrooms, or man who chases another man through the home in a fit of anger. My mother used to tell me and my brothers the story of how when she was a teenager, she would watch a ghostly woman appear in her bedroom night after night at midnight. The woman would open the window seal each night and then jump to her death only to disappear when she hit the ground.

A psychic echo, sometimes called a psychic imprint, is a spiritual phenomenon where the same short event is repeated night after night. This is not the actual spirit of the deceased person, but rather a psychic flash of the event of what happened long ago. What happens is that when a strong emotion accompanies a traumatic event it leaves an energetic reverberation on the astral and etheric planes. Even when a death is not involved, strong emotions can still be felt in a room. How many times have you walked into a room and you can still feel the energies from someone who is just in a heated argument? With the added traumatic energies of a death, then the reverberation is greatly increased and leaves the energies to be a sort of energetic video recorder that is set to play at the exact time the event happened. A human haunting does not repeat the same event night after night. They get our attention in a variety of ways and cause physical manifestations such as objects moving. When the Psychopomp engages with a psychic echo there is no engagement back where a human haunting will almost always engage back in some way.

Psychic echoes can be taken care of relatively easily most of the time. When cleansing a psychic echo there are a few things to keep in mind. See if there is a spiritual power source that is feeding the energetic recording. You will have to energetically "plug" up the energy or reroute it some way. You can banish the echo by taking one of your spiritual tools, such as an athame, stang, crystal, or wand and blasting it with spiritual power. You can also energetically sweep or scoop the energy into a sacred vessel such as a magical mojo bag or box and discard the energy outside. You can bury it or discard it in moving water. I have been known to use my bare hands with this type of cleansing. I focus my mind to tune into the specific plane or dimension the echo is manifesting on and scoop it with my hands and then place it outside of the home. Then I spiritually cleanse the home.

Dark Hauntings

In movies about hauntings, they are always telling us a story about the evil ghosts who scare the unsuspecting homeowners out. Some movies and TV shows about hauntings go so far and show spirits killing people. In shows like *The Amityville Horror* or *American Horror Story* we see vindictive ghosts hellbent on revenge or the lust for blood. Even though this is a good scare, this is extremely rare. Most of the hauntings that you will be called to are usually lost or confused spirits who need guidance and spiritual help in some way. Most of the spirits you will encounter cannot manifest the energy needed to physically harm someone or pick up a dangerous tool. However, as rare as it is, it can happen. There are spirits, who in life, were murderers and psychopaths. Remember, when you die you do not automatically become healed and enlightened. When you die, you are detaching from your physical body. Who you are emotionally, mentally, and energetically remains the same. If you were a bad person in life, you will be a bad person in the afterlife.

There have been a few times in my career as a psychopomp that I have encountered spirits such as this. From my experience with them, they were not able to physically hurt me or hurl a knife at me. They did not have the energetic strength to do so. What they *could* do is change the energy in the home to such a negative feel that everyone in the home either wanted to get out or felt extremely nauseous and sick. I remember feeling so much hate and anger that I had to use extra magical protection and even then, I could feel the energy trying to get through my shields. Normally, I tell my students to stay calm and maintain the healer's mindset of compassion, but in this case, it is time to be super witch.

Allow me to take a moment and explain what this means. Negative spirits feed off of your fear just as a bully would feed off of the fear of someone who is afraid of them. The bully thinks they have control in the situation. It is true that if you are afraid, your energy shields and wards will become weak and then you will become vulnerable. When you encounter dark spirits, demons, or monsters, it is important that you have the magical confidence to handle any situation or else you should not be in that situation. If I have to, I can take my magical dagger and banish dark spirits to the deepest part of the Underworld without hesitation or regret.

In the cases with someone who is mentally unstable, they will also have the same mentality after they transition into death. This can be very troubling because it is very unfair that the poor soul who spent their life suffering must now also spend their afterlife suffering. As a healer, I would love to think that I could send the spirit healing energy and then escort them to the realm of the ancestors. This is one of those times that it is not so cut and dry. They may respond to energy healing well or they may reject it. Yes, people can reject energy healing if they want. Also, they may need much more energy healing than we are able to give. In hauntings where a mentally unstable person had died, it can feel very unstable. Just like with angry spirits, mentally unstable spirits rarely can affect the physical plane but are able to affect the energy in the home instead. The experiences with these types of spirits I had the feelings of dizziness, confusion, and sometimes panic. I did not allow myself to take on these energies, but I could feel them in the room. The spirit was transferring their own emotions and thoughts into the home and everyone else was able to feel these energies as well.

What if you do not have a lot of experience with spirits? I learned advanced psychic self-defense from my magical teachers, shamans, and other witches through many years of study. I also learned from my Psychopomp Teacher as well as my ancestral teachers and guides. Working with your Psychopomp Teacher is far better than any other human teacher you could ever hope for. Human teachers are important though. They can help you troubleshoot situations from a human perspective that is very valuable. In the rest of this chapter, I will teach you some really good psychic self-defense techniques that will be very beneficial to your magical work with spirits. Until you become proficient at these psychic self-defense techniques, I will advise that if you get called to a home with dark spirits you should seek out psychopomps or witches who have more experience dealing with things like this.

Non-Human Hauntings

There are many things in the energy worlds besides the spirits of the dead and the gods. I am often called to the homes of magical people because they know that I am experienced with the three shamanic worlds and I can handle whatever spiritual problem that arises. One of the most common things that happens when someone journeys into the three worlds, especially the Underworld, is that they may accidentally bring something back with them. Most of the time, these entities are harmless and are attracted to your energy for some reason. More often than not, they see your energy as bright and healing and they are attracted to it, like a puppy following you home. If this is the case, all you need to do is open a portal with your wand or athame and visualize the entity going back to where it came. You can also ask your guides to take it back home where it will be safe.

Another common spirit that causes disturbances in the home are the elves and faeries. In my book, *Otherworld: Ecstatic Witchcraft for the Spirits of the Land,* I talk about how homes are sometimes built on faery roads and they have no qualms about traipsing through your home causing havoc. During faery nights, you can open the front and back doors allowing the train of the fey to march forth through your home on the way to whatever it is faeries do in secret on faery nights. My best advice is to journey to the home of the faeries or elves and ask to speak with whomever is leading the faery train. Give them offerings of gifts and food and with courtesy ask them if it is possible to adjust their faery roads so as to not disturb the home. If this is not agreeable, ask them for some compromise that will benefit both parties. The fey are more understanding than you may think.

I have also been called to someone's home because they conjured something they could not put back. As a teacher, this is frustrating. Anyone who has read my books knows that I hate gatekeeping. That being said, there is something to be said about not performing advanced works of magick until you are ready. You should not call upon a goetic demon or a dark spirit just to see if you can. Conjuring spirits is not necessarily hard, but controlling the spirit and putting it back where it came from is an entirely different matter. I will never tell someone they cannot do an act of magick, but I will say practice all the beginning techniques on magick first before you try conjunctions. If you do find yourself taking magical risks and not listening to your teachers, here are a few hints to help you. First, anything that you conjure, reverse the wording to send it back. So instead of saying, "I call you spirit" say instead, "I send you back to where you came. May you cause no harm on your return." Make sure you have your wards and protective shields upon yourself and your temple space. It should go without saying that you should never do conjunctions when you are intoxicated, angry, or depressed. Like attracts like and you may summon negative energies to your temple space.

Spiritual Diagnosis of the Home

Before any kind of work can begin in someone's home. There are a few things you will need to do to prepare. The first thing you will need to do is speak with everyone involved. Get to know each person. Find out what they do for a living. What kind of daily stressors do they have? Do they have a job that they love, or do they wake up each day wishing there were more out of life? See where I am going with this? Sometimes, people are seeking excitement in their life to take them out of the ordinary everyday humdrum. I have seen on occasion where someone's fantasy life takes over them and they see a haunting when there is none. Sometimes an old house is just a creaky old house. The next thing you will need to do is find out how their relationships are and family dynamic. Is there violence in the home or is it a healthy loving environment? Also, find out if they are magical or not. You will be surprised to find that people who have never thought of magick can have a lot of psychic ability. There is an interesting anomaly that involves poltergeist which means *noisy ghost.* In a poltergeist haunting, objects move around and doors and drawers open and close. As much as this looks like a sure sign of a haunting it is actually the product of repressed telekinetic powers that have no outlet to manifest so they begin to manifest their telekinetic ability subconsciously. Dishes will move, chairs will be in a different place, and lights will flicker. All of these are classic symptoms of a haunting, but in reality, the person in question is unknowingly making these things happen.

You will need to find out as much history on the home as possible. Ask the residents what they know about the prior occupants of the home. As "un-witchy" as it might sound, Google can be a valuable tool with magick. See what you can find out about the address, prior residence, and the land on which the house or apartment building was built. Was there a home prior to the current one on the property? Are there any outstanding events that show up? One of the things I find myself doing is Googling the address of the haunting and the keywords "crime", "death", "violence", to see if anything comes up. Sometimes you get lucky and find an old newspaper article about it and sometimes you do not. You will have to find the history of the home the old-fashioned way, your own psychic powers.

Once you have taken an intake on the residence and the history of the home you will need to use your psychic skills and assess the energies of the home itself. Walk through each room one by one in a gentle and non-threatening way. You may be a powerful witch, but this is not the time to show off that power. Remember to maintain the mindset of the healer. Spirits can sense your energies and if you are aggressive or hostile in any way, they may not show themselves to you and then you will not be able to help them transition. When I enter a home that may be haunted, I try to manifest the energies of compassion and healing so that the spirits know that I am there to help them and not harm in anyway. Look at the physical condition of the home. Is it clean in good condition or is it falling apart with clear signs of neglect? A dirty and broken-down home can lend itself to energies that have lower vibrations.

Before you begin, call upon your gods, Psychopomp Teacher, and guides. Ask them to protect and guide you. Center and shield as you normally would. As you enter each room you will need to use your psychic senses and perceive the energies that are manifesting. Every room will carry a psychic echo of the past events that once occurred. The stronger the emotion that is connected with the past event the stronger you will be able to perceive what happened. You will use a psychic skill that is closely related to psychometry, but instead of picking up an object and reading the energies, you will read the energies in the room. Zak Bagans explains in his book, *Dark World: Into the Shadows with Lead Investigator of the Ghost Adventures Crew,* about how he was able to psychically connect to the place where a murder took place. He says:

> "I had an immediate and powerful emotional connection to the place where she died. The room looked different. My ears rang. I could smell something being cooked in the kitchen down the hall and I saw flash images of her life...in that moment I felt like I was there when Preston Castle and Anna Corbin were both alive and well."

Performing this type of psychic work is relatively easy. You just have to not only know *how* to do it but know it *can* be done.

1. Stand in the center of the room. If it helps you focus you may close your eyes. Take a few deep breaths and center yourself into the space.

2. Reach out with both your heart and your mind at the same time. Become aware of your Sphere of Sensation. Know that the Sphere of Sensation has the power to see all things past, present, and future. Expand your sphere to encompass the entire room.

3. Allow the Sphere of Sensation to pick up all the energies in the room. Allow the energies to fill your heart and mind with what happened in the past. Make sure you stay centered. This type of psychic work can leave you feeling very spacey.

4. What images are you seeing? Can you see them clearly? If not, ask your spirits and guides to help manifest the pictures in a clear way that you can understand.

5. If you need, you can go deeper with your mind to find things further in the past. Imagine yourself and your

psychic sphere traveling into the past to where the situation that caused the haunting to happen. Think of it like scrying into a magick bowl or magick mirror, but instead of a scrying bowl you are scrying into the room itself.

6. Even though your mind and heart travels back in time, know that your body remains in the present.

7. Decipher the images and information to the best of your ability. When you are ready, take a deep breath and return to your body in the present. Ground and center as needed.

When you practice this technique, over time, you will be able to walk into any room and get a read on it. You can use this same technique to pick up spiritual energies that are in the present too. Meaning, you can use this to find any spirits of the dead who are trying to hide from you. Some spirits will know immediately why you are there. To them, you are going to evict them from their chosen place of occupancy, and they may try to hide their energy signature so that you will not be able to detect them. This technique will help you find any energy that you are looking for.

Cleansing the Home

Before you can do any of the footwork with hauntings you will need to cleanse the home. When we are energetically cleansing someone's home, we are not banishing any of the spirits at this time. What we are doing is cleansing the extra energy that may impede or contaminate our spiritual work. Spirits emit energy just as living people do. This is one of the reasons we are able to feel their presence. When a spirit has negative emotions, they will fill the home with that energy. Also, the living people inside the home are contributing to the negative energy at times. There may be days, weeks, or even months of the energetic buildup of stress, negative thoughts, anger, etc. from just the mere fact that someone's house is haunted. If you were not magical and your house was being plagued by dark scary spirits, wouldn't you be stressed out? This negative energy builds up over time and we will need to energetically clean the space so we can do our psychopomp work in a positive and therapeutic manner. Think of it as a doctor cleaning the mud and dirt off of a deep cut so they can stitch you back together again.

There are many ways you can cleanse the home. You can use a smudge or fumigation, energy wipe down, or a psychic cleansing. I do not recommend a house blessing until the house is cleansed and the spirits have been taken care of.

Smudging/ Fumigation

Smudging and fumigation are the same thing. They both involve using herbs and resins to energetically cleanse a space. In the United States, smudging has come to mean the use of sage, tobacco, sweetgrass, or cedar. All of these plants grow naturally in the U.S., so it makes sense to use the herbs that we have. As always, we must respect the spirit of the planets in order for them to work to their highest good. If you are going to use a fumigation you can use any herb or resin that has a spiritually high vibration such as frankincense, mugwort, juniper, rosemary, and many others.

1. Place your herbs in a fire-proof vessel.
2. Place your hand over the herbs. Bring your consciousness to the celestial realms of creation, protection, and spirit. As you inhale, draw down the magical power of the heavens into your crown chakra and then to your heart. I like to visualize this energy as a powerful white light from the gods. On the exhale, send the energies of cleansing and protection from your heart, through your hands and into the plant. See the plant retain this

magical power.

3. Light the herb in the vessel. As the smoke rises, see the magical power of the celestial light emanating from the plant.

4. Walk clockwise around each room in the home. Normally, when I banish, I like to go counterclockwise, but in this case, I like to go with the movement of the sun because I am drawing on the energy of balance and harmony while I am doing my cleansing.

5. Remember this is a gentle cleansing. You do not want to be aggressive with the cleansing by smoke, so you do not upset the spirit(s). If you upset the spirits, they may become harder to work with later.

6. Leave the remainder of the herbs outside as an offering to the nature spirits. Leaving the smudge inside will leave the home too smokey.

Energy Wipe Down

An energy wipe down is where you focus on the negative energy in the home and use the natural magnetism of your hands to "wipe down" the energy of each room. This is more time consuming than smudging and takes more psychic focus. You will need to make sure you wipe down all the walls and furniture in each room.

1. Close your eyes for a moment and call upon your gods, guides, and Pychopomp Teacher. With your heart and your mind, summon them into the space you are working.

2. Bring your consciousness to the celestial heavens. Inhale and bring the powerful cleansing energies of the stars and galaxies down to your crown chakra and into your heart.

3. Now, ask your gods, teachers, and guides to send you

energy and power so you may clean the home. With an exhaled breath, send the power of the heavens and your spirits into your hand. Sense your hands glowing with cleansing magical power.

4. You will not need to physically "wash" each wall and each piece of furniture. You can gesture a sweeping motion over each wall and each piece of furniture. Visualize a very large sized sphere emanating from your hands that is able to clear the entire wall.

5. Again, remember that this is a gentle cleansing. Center and ground as needed.

Psychic Cleansing

This technique draws upon the power of your psychic mind. It uses your own personal psychic force to cleans any unwanted energy out of each room.

1. Stand at the doorway of the room.
2. Close your eyes, open your arms wide, and energetically connect to the space of the room. Connect to the four walls, the ceiling, and the floor.
3. Open your heart chakra and connect to the energies of the room. Do not take any of the negative energy into you. You are sensing the energies, nothing more.
4. Take a deep breath and on the exhale, visualize and sense a strong gale blowing through the room. As the great wind blows, all negative energy is blown away from the home.
5. Perform in each room until the house is completely cleansed. Center and ground and usual.

Spirit Attachments

Before we go into releasing and banishing unwanted ghosts, I would like to talk a little about spirit attachments. Spirit attachments sometimes cause nightmares and a feeling of being watched. The person never truly feels alone. They may also sometimes experience aches and sharp pains in the body. This is due to the spirit trying to absorb the person's life force. When these symptoms occur, some people think they are being haunted by a ghost. A spirit attachment is a spirit that has a very low vibration. Think of them as astral mosquitoes that feed on human life force. Many spirit attachments are nothing more than thought forms that have taken up a life of their own. Thought forms are created all the time. Anytime we give energy to any thought at all it becomes a thought form. Most of the time thought forms do not have the energy to sustain themselves so they wither away back into the astral. However, in places with a lot of stress and negativity they can become semi self-aware. Think about places where negative energy can become congested such as a large city or a home that has trauma and abuse. These thought forms need a human host to gain energy from. They will then create a tendril into the chakras and aura of a person. Some of the signs of a spirit attachment are:

1. Feeling constantly tired or lethargic
2. Lowered immune system leading to sickness
3. Depression
4. Feeling of hopeless or helplessness
5. Diminished personal Will
6. Feeling worthless or unloved

These symptoms do not automatically mean that the person has a spiritual attachment. You will need to use your psychic vision to assess if there is one or not. If you are still developing your psychic sight, close your eyes and visualize the person standing in front of you. Use your astral eyes in your meditation to see if there are any spirit attachments or negative energies around the person. If they do have a spirit attachment, determine if it is a thought form or another form of entity. If it is a thought form it usually appears as larva or a mass of some sort without any real form. One of the easiest ways to banish thought form larva is to use your magical dagger or knife and "pop" the creature. Thought forms are very weak so this should do the trick. Use your visualization skills to see any tendrils left going into the chakras. Take your hands and pull them out. Throw them on the ground to be naturally absorbed by the earth. Touching them with your hands will not hurt you.

If you find that the spirit is not a thought form and it is either a human spirit or another type of spirit, you will need to release the spirit from the person and send it to where it needs to be.

For a Human Spirit:

1. Call upon your gods, guides, and Psychopomp Teacher.
2. With your clairvoyance, determine where the spirit is attaching itself to the living host. Most of the time it will either be attached from the back of the person at the heart or solar plexus. These two chakras are very powerful and give spirits a lot of energy to feed on.
3. With a magical dagger or just your finger, cut the astral chord between the spirit and the living person.
4. As with other psychopomp ceremonies, listen to the spirit's story and explain to them in the best way possible that they will be happier and healthier with their ancestors and will receive the healing they need.
5. Send the spirit healing energy. Most likely, the reason they were attached to a living person to begin with, is because they are out of balance or spiritually unhealthy in some way.
6. Call upon the spirit's ancestors. You may also ask your gods and guides to go to the Underworld and find the ancestors for you.
7. The spirit's ancestors may escort them home. But if the

spirit resists or is afraid, you may need to escort the spirit yourself.

8. Once the spirit is home, send healing energy to the living person so they may heal from any energy wounds inflicted by the spirit.

For Other Spirits

There are many spirits in the three worlds, and some of them, who are unbalanced, may attach themselves to a person who has a weak aura and energy body. The magical technique to get rid of them is similar to the above but with a few adjustments.

1. Call upon your gods, guides, and Psychopomp Teacher.
2. With your clairvoyance, determine where the spirit is attaching itself to the living host. Most of the time it will either be attached from the back of the person at the heart or solar plexus. These two chakras are very powerful and give spirits a lot of energy to feed on.
3. With a magical dagger, or just your finger, cut the astral chord between the spirit and the living person.
4. If you have experience with different types of spirits, you should be able to determine what type of spirit you have encountered. If you are unsure, ask your gods and guides for the identity of the spirit. Spirits who feed off the lifeforce of the living are unbalanced and you will most likely not convince them to leave the human host alone. My recommendation is to ask your gods, guides, and Psychopomp to take the spirit to a place where it can get the healing it needs. They will be able to take the spirit to a place that is better suited for it.
5. Once the spirit is gone, send healing energy to the living person so that any wounds in their aura, chakras, or energy bodies will be healed.

Weak Energies, Weak Boundaries

Spirit attachments usually only happen when someone has a weak aura and energy body. When someone is under a lot of stress or trauma their energies become weaker. Their aura shrinks and does not have a strong emanation of life force. The aura is the first protective shield from spirit attachments. When it is strong and glowing, it radiates a bright energy that repels spirits who have a low vibration in the same way as a blast of white spiritual light repels lower spirits. This can happen to even the most skilled witch or Spirit Walker. It has even happened to me from time to time. Having a spirit attachment does not mean you have little power as a witch. On the contrary, it means that you have run yourself into the ground for whatever reason and your energies have become depleted. I know so many people who work several jobs plus maintain a magical practice. It is a wonder more people do not have spirit attachments. For self-care, I ask my gods to remove any energy attachments and to send me healing energy to strengthen my energies. Luckily, we witches have our gods, ancestors, and guides to help us with this. Not everyone has this luxury.

As always, when removing spirit attachments, keep the healer's mindset and do not judge a person for having an attachment. Like I said, it happens to powerful witches too, not just non-magical people. One thing we can teach people is to make sure they have strong healthy boundaries. Healthy boundaries do not mean being angry at someone every time they cross us or do something we do not like. Healthy boundaries mean that hold strong in our personal power, Will, and decisions in the face of adversary or dissenting opinion. It also means that we have our own personal code of ethics that we hold on to and do not change who we are because someone else thinks we should.

Another thing we have to sometimes teach people is the 'victim mentality'. Let us talk about this for a moment. Being the victim of a crime, trauma, or abuse is not the same thing as victim mentality. Victim mentality means that a person feels that they are the target of trauma or abuse when there is no trauma or abuse. It is also the idea that "bad stuff" always happens to them. Some people who have a victim mentality have poor boundaries and are easily influenced by others. There is much more to the victim mentality than what I am expressing here, but it gives you the general idea. If you can encourage someone who exhibits these signs to speak to someone who will be able to help them. In my experience, many people who have these thought patterns open themselves up to spirit attachments. You can give them protective amulets and charms, but at the end of the day, it is up to each of us to seek the help we need to have a healthy and balanced life.

Hauntings of the Mentally Insane

It does not happen very often, but occasionally you may run into a haunting by a spirit who is mentally insane. This can occur in mental hospitals, prisons, and sometimes someone's home. There are many types of mental illness. Some illnesses are mild while others are very severe. Mental illness can manifest itself a wide variety of ways. Sometimes a spirit may become obsessed with someone in the home and they do not want them to associate with any other person. Other times, the spirit can become violent and cause physical objects to move. They have occasionally been known to attack people. This manifests as bite marks, scratches, bruises, and other physical wounds. One of the more common things insane spirits do is influence the living to have the same mental illness as they do.

As we talked about before, the spirits can influence the energetic environment in the home or building and this can slowly influence our minds. Most of the time we do not even notice this is happening. A sure sign you are being influenced by a spirit is if you are showing mental instability in a home or building and as soon as you leave you feel back to normal.

Some people may have nightmares of the spirit doing horrible things or attacking them. The cases I have seen where there was a haunting by an insane spirit, the spirit did not realize they were influencing the occupants of the home. Insane spirits do not always realize how powerful their energetic influence is and may not be intentionally trying to influence the living.

The occupants of the home may also see psychic echoes of the insane spirit. Sometimes in jails or hospitals, a psychically sensitive person may see scenes of the person in life attacking or killing someone. They may even see the person screaming in anger and causing violence against others.

Unfortunately, what we consider hauntings are usually done by mentally ill and unstable spirits. That being said, there are aggressive spirits who are not insane that are incredibly angry that cause hauntings as well. There is often a rage or obsession that the insane spirit has latched on to and cannot let go. Most spirits that we help heal and guide to the ancestral realm have a reason, no matter how small, to stay on the physical plane. Insane spirits may not have the cognizant skills to realize they have died, and they need to move on to the Land of the Ancestors and find healing with the helping and healing spirits. Sadly, when their ancestors come to take them to the Land of the Ancestors the spirit may be confused and angry and does not understand what is happening to them. This is very sad, indeed. Not only do they have mental illness in life that is causing them harm, they are also suffering in death and do not understand they will be better in the afterlife.

I must make it clear that not all mentally insane people have this situation upon their death. In my experience, I have only seen the hauntings by mentally unstable spirits who are very angry and are criminally insane. All these spirits understand is anger and confusion and it is very difficult to help them. I do not recommend for the beginner psychopomp healer to work with these spirits until they are well experienced. If your

Psychopomp Teacher and healing gods recommend that you work with these spirits for healing then it is vital that you do exactly what they say. In fact, I would recommend that the first few times you do this work you allow the Psychopomp Teacher to take the lead and you observe until you get a handle on what is needed for this type of work.

You will find at times that you cannot heal certain spirits of the dead. It saddens me to say that there are a few rare times that you will need to banish the spirit so that they can no longer harm living people. After you have done everything you can and you have spoken at length to your Psychopomp Teacher and the gods, you will have to aggressively banish the astral body of the spirit to free their spiritual body in order for them to receive the healing that they need in the Land of the Ancestors. Once again, I would only banish the spirit only after you spoke to Psychopomp Teachers and your gods.

Banishing a Spirit

As psychopomps we are healers. Throughout this book It is my sincere hope that you see the work that we do as healing and transformative for both the spirits of the dead and for you. I have said it many times and I would like to say it once more, we have to approach the spirits of the dead with compassion and kindness. However, you may encounter a spirit that is causing harm, which can come in many different ways. It is a rare occasion that a spirit has the energy to cause physical harm to someone. Rare, but it does happen. The harm I have encountered a spirit do is more mental, emotional, and astral. It is very sad to realize that when some people die who are insane or criminals, they do not become healthy balanced people simply because they have died. It takes a lot of time and learning with the spirit healers and guides for that to happen. This is why it is so important to help the dead crossover to the afterlife. It is only there where they will find the healing they need.

Harm from the spirit of the dead can come in a variety of ways. If they are causing disturbances in the home this can cause a lot of anguish and grief to the living and cause mental and emotional harm. When a spirit is invading someone's dreams, this can also cause mental and emotional harm. Astral harm can come from a spirit attaching itself to a person and feeding off their life force. Unbalanced spirits can also change the energy in a room and even the entire home. They have the ability to manipulate the energy in such a way that it becomes energetically toxic to all concerned. I have encountered many unbalanced spirits who have caused people to harm each other and themselves simply by changing the energy in the room to that of violence and hate.

It is far better to try to reason with the spirit and try to give them healing energy, but sometimes this does not help. Even unbalanced spirits have the choice of free will. They do not have to do anything they do not want to. In fact, some imbalanced spirits may not even understand that they are causing harm to the living and other spirits. When all else has failed, you may have no choice but to banish a spirit from the physical plane. In order to do this, you will need your magical dagger or wand. We will summon a great amount of spiritual energy and destroy the astral body causing a second death. The second death, normally, is when a spirit naturally sheds its astral body and is in the form of pure spirit. This happens when a spirit has evolved beyond needing an astral body and can join the ancestors in a deeper, spiritual way. They are no longer bound by the trappings of the astral body. Each person's astral body contains our emotions, memories, hopes and fears, imagination, and our personal will. I know this sounds very traumatic but if a person's astral body has become so contaminated with the energies of rage, revenge, sickness, hate and mental instability, it is far better to help them shed the astral body that has become sick. Think of it like amputating a limb that has become necrotic and the only way to save a person's life is to get rid of the toxic limb. That being said, I would never do an aggressive banishing such as this without consulting my gods, guides, ancestors, and Psychopomp Teacher. They may have a better solution for all concerned. But they may not.

Before you begin, I would recommend energetically cleansing the living people involved and sending them away for the duration of the ritual. They need to be cleansed and checked for attachments; because if the spirit knows what you are about to do, they may attach to the living person and follow them out.

Items needed:

Magical dagger or wand
Quartz crystals or regular stones
Protective talismans

1. Place your protective talismans around your neck. It should be long enough to go over your heart. This will protect you from the influence of the hostile spirit. You can use a charged pentacle or other symbol that is sacred to you. Shield yourself and make sure your shield is extra strong. You can invoke protective angels, gods, spirits, or place protective symbols around your shield such as pentacles.

2. Before you begin, call upon your gods, ancestors, guides, and Psychopomp Teacher to assist you in this ritual. You may call the spirit's ancestors to assist or to be present during the process. You will need to explain the situation to them, so they understand why you are doing the banishing.

3. With your crystals or stones, create a magical circle about 2.5 feet in diameter. Just large enough for a grown person to stand in. You will be standing outside of the circle. It is meant to contain the hostile spirit. Take your

magical dagger or wand and draw a powerful blue circle over the stones. This will add to the power of the circle so that it fully contains the spirit.

4. Place the magical dagger or wand behind you on a small table out of sight of the spirit. If the spirit sees it during the ritual, it may become even more hostile.

5. Ask your ancestors and guides to find the spirit's ancestors in the ancestral lands. When they arrive, explain the situation to them. Most likely they already know, but out of courtesy make sure they understand. When the astral body of the spirit is shed, they will need to take the spirit to a place of healing.

6. Call upon the hostile spirit. Ideally, you will have the spirit's name, but if not, you can visualize how the spirit appears to you with your clairvoyant vision. Visualize the spirit manifesting in the circle of stones. Know with all your being and magick that the circle of stones contains the spirit.

7. Take your dagger or wand with both hands. Extend it, tip pointing up to the heavens. With an inhale, draw down the supercharged power of the universe in a beam of white light. Point the weapon toward the spirit and take a deep breath. With your powerful magical Will, take another breath and on the exhale yell, "GO!" and see a powerful white light shoot from your weapon and vaporize the astral body of the spirit leaving only the pure spirit.

8. Ask the spirit's ancestors to take the spirit back to the realm of the ancestors for healing. Thank them for their presence. Open a portal with your weapon and visualize them going through with the spirit.

9. Thank your gods, ancestors, guides, and Psychopomp Teacher.

10. Banish any residual energies as you normally would.

Closing Entrances and Portals

Once you have cleared the home of all unwanted energies, attachments, and spirits you will need to close up any energy entrances or portals that spirits will be able to use to come back in the home. If you are very psychically sensitive, you will be able to feel them while you are examining the home. You can also use your clairvoyant abilities and find them in the astral.

1. Place yourself in a light trance state.
2. Walk through the entirety of the home examining closets, windows, corners, ceilings, etc.
3. While in each room, close your eyes and visualize the room. Do you see any energy entrances or portals that may allow spirits to come through?
4. In order to close the portals you find, take your dagger or wand and draw universal energy into it. Then, point the tip of the weapon at the entrance and draw an energetic line of white light that is sealing up the entrance. Know that the powerful light of the universe is sealing it shut.
5. If the portal feels especially strong you may place added power over the seal with rune such as algiz, a pentacle, an "x", or any other spiritual symbol that feels powerful to you.
6. It is also wise to place protective talismans in the windows and over the front and back doors of the home.

Wards and Shields

You will need to teach the residents of the home how to ward and shield their home. This will protect the home long after you have cleared it from unwanted energies and it gives those living in the home a sense of control over their own environment. If you went to someone's home for a haunting, then odds are they believe in some sort of higher power. You should have them call upon that higher power first. If they do not have a definition of what that higher power is, then just the Universe will do. Have the occupants pray to their higher power for peace, love, and protection in the home. They will then need to go to front and back doors and energetically place a symbol over the front and back doors. If they are magically inclined, they can use the rune algiz or a pentacle. If they are Christian, they can certainly place the sign of the cross over the doors. If not, they can draw an "x" instead. Once that is done, have them visualize the Universe filling their home with powerful loving and protective light. Next, they should visualize a giant protective sphere encasing their entire home. This should be done every night before they go to bed.

You can place magical charms around the home to add further protection. Make sure that the charms are magically charged to protect the home from spiritual intrusion of all types. You can use crystals, herbs, horseshoes, mojo bags, nails, and other magical items to keep unwanted energies out of the home. One of my favorite charms is to take two pieces of rowan wood and bind it with red string to form a cross. This can be hung in your window or doorway to keep negative energies out. You can also create a magical tincture of protective herbs, dip a cloth in it, and wipe down the window and door seals in your home.

The best thing I have found to keep the home safe from spiritual intrusions and hauntings is to have a regular spiritual practice which include honoring the gods and especially honoring the ancestors. The ancestors will be able to protect your home very well from unwanted energies. Every single night I place energy wards over my doors to keep negative energies out. I then ask the ancestors to protect my home and all who live within its walls. I see all of my ancestors in my heart and then visualize them going back through the generations surrounding my home. As I visualize the ancestors protecting my home, I can see the magical energy of love and protection circling around the home, keeping myself and my loved one safe from all harm. By keeping the energies in the home flowing with love, compassion, and healing vibrations, it will be very well protected. You can also ask your gods, ancestors, and Psychopomp Teacher for further ways to keep the good energy flowing in the home.

Self-Care

When you are asked to take care of a haunting it can be both an empowering and draining experience at the same time. You will need to use many of your psychic talents in order to help the spirit move on to the afterlife. Many times, you will feel invigorated and connected to the universe. Other times, you may feel very drained of your energy. This is ok. It can sometimes happen that you use a lot of your energy in order to clear someone's home of unwanted spirits and other psychic phenomenon. Just as with all magick, you will need to take an opportunity to take care of yourself. Remember, when you are clearing a space from unwanted hauntings, make especially sure you are connecting to your Psychopomp Teacher and listening to their guidance. And of course, you will have the assistance of your gods and guides as well. They will help you in not exerting too much of your own energy. But if you do, it is ok. When you return home, make sure that you are doing basic energy cleansing on yourself. You should also make sure you eat and drink plenty of water. I know this sounds very beginner level, but when your energies are zapped out even the best of us forget to take care of ourselves. I would also suggest not engaging in any more magick for the night as well. Sometimes a night by the television is the best you can do for yourself after using heavy amounts of magick and psychic power. Make sure you are listening to your body and your spirit. Be kind and patient with yourself.

Conclusion

Death is the final rite of passage of our physical life. As we know, death is not the end. There is a spiritual journey ahead for each person. Each of us must walk our own path of death and into the realm of the afterlife. Walking our spiritual path at death can be difficult and we may need the help of a guide. The psychopomp has the sacred duty of guiding the spirits of the dead back home to be with their beloved ancestors. There are many times in life where people need healing. So, too, it is in death. The act of dying can be very frightening to people and they may need our help in this transition into spirit. They may also need our help find their way home. It is a privilege to be able to assist the spirits in their journey into the spiritual planes.

Being a psychopomp is a very humbling experience. It is not about power or doing magick to shape the universe by our will. It is about assisting someone in need. It is about listening to our spirit teachers so that we can become better healers to the spirits. It is about taking a frightened person by the hand and leading them to a place of healing. Being a psychopomp is about supporting someone who no longer has their physical life and being present for this great transition. Being a psychopomp is being a healer.

Bibliography

Ahern, June. *How To Speak With Spirits: Seances-Mediums-Ghost Hunts.* CreateSpace. 2017.

Allaun, Chris. *Deeper Into The Underworld: Death, Ancestors, and Magical Rites.* Mandrake of Oxford. 2017.

Allaun, Chris. *Otherworld: Ecstatic Witchcraft for the Spirits of the Land.* Moon Books. 2020.

Allaun, Chris. *Underworld: Shamanism, Myth, and Magick.* Mandrake of Oxford. 2016.

Allaun, Chris. *Upperworld: Shamanism and Magick of the Celestial Realm.* Mandrake of Oxford. 2019.

Bagans, Zak. Kelly, Crigger. *Dark World: Into The Shadows With The Lead Investigator of the Ghost Adventures Crew.* Victor Belt Publishing. 2010.

Belanger, Michelle. *The Ghost Hunter's Survival Guide: Protection Techniques For Encounters With The Paranormal.* Llewellyn Worldwide. 2009.

Belanger, Michelle. *The Psychic Energy Codex: Awakening Your Subtle Senses.* Weiser Books. 2007.

Betty, Stafford Ph.D. *The Afterlife Unveiled: What the Dead are Telling Us About Their World.* 6th Books. 2011.

Brannen, Cyndi. *Keeping Her Keys: An Introduction to Hekate's Modern Witchcraft.* Moon Books. 2019.

Bulfinch, Thomas. *Myths of Greece and Rome.* Penguin Books. 1979.

Carabas, Markus. *Anubis: The History and Legacy of the Ancient Egyptian God of the Afterlife.* Charles Rivers Editors. 2018.

Chesnut, R. Andrew. *Devoted To Death: Santa Muerte The Skeleton Saint.* Oxford University Press. 2018.

Chia, Mantak. *Healing Light of the Tao: Foundational Practices to Awaken Chi Energy.* Destiny Books. 2008.

Coleman, Martin. *Communing With The Spirits.* Samuel Weiser, Inc. 1998.

Davidson, Gustav. *A Dictionary of Angel Including The Fallen Angels.* Free Press. 1967.

D' Este, Sorita. *Circle For Hekate: Volume I: History and Mythology.* Avalonia. 2017.

D'Este, Sorita and David Rankine. *Hekate Liminal Rites: A Study of the Rituals, Magic and Symbols of the Torch-Bearing Triple Goddess of the Crossroads.* Avalonia. 2011, 2019.

Devereux, Paul. *Spirit Roads: An Exploration of Otherworldly Routes.* Collins and Brown. 2003.

Dillard, Sherrie. *You Are A Medium: Discover Your Natural Abilities to Communicate With The Otherside.* Llewellyn Publications. 2013.

Dominguez, Ivo, Jr. *Spirit Speak: Knowing and Understanding Spirit Guides, Ancestors, Ghosts, Angels, and the Divine.* New Page Books. 2008.

Filan, Kenaz. *The Haitian Vodou Handbook: Protocols for Riding with the Lwa.* Destiny Books. 2006.

Forest, Danu. *Pagan Portals: Gwyn Ap Nudd: Wild God of Faerie Guardian of Annwfn.* Moon Books. 2017.

Fortune, Dion. *Psychic Self-Defense.* Weiser Books. 2011.

Fortune, Dion. *Through The Gates of Death.* Ariel Press. 2013.

Glassman, Sallie Ann. *Vodou Visions: An Encounter With Divine Mystery.* Garrett County Press. 2014.

Grant, Robert J. *The Place We Call Home: Exploring The Soul's Existence After Death.* Hart Warming Classics. 2019.

Herman, Stephen A. *Medium Mastery The Ultimate Guide: The Mechanics of Receiving Spirit Communications.* Atendriya Press. 2015.

Johnston, Sarah Iles. *Restless Dead: Encounters Between the Living and the Dead in Ancient Greece.* University of California Press. 1999.

Jung, C.G. Translated by R. F. C. Hull. *The Collected Works of C.G. Jung: Volume 9ii: Aion: Researches Into The Phenomenology of the Self.* Princeton University Press. 1959, 1979.

Kaldera, Raven. *The Pathwalker's Guide To The Nine Worlds.*

Asphodel Press. 2006.

Kerenyi, Karl. *Hermes: Guide of Souls.* Spring Publications. 2015.

Kowalewski, David, PhD. *Death Walkers: Shamanic Psychopomps, Earthbound Ghosts, and Helping Spirits in the Afterlife Realm.* iUniverse. 2015.

Rinponche, Khenchen Palden Sherab and Khendpo Tsewang Dongyal Rinpoche. *The Essential Journey of Life and Death: Volume 1: The Indestructible Nature of Body, Speech, and Mind.* Dharma Samudra. 2012.

Madden, Kristin. *Shamanic Guide To Death and Dying.* Llewellyn Publications. 1999.

McCarthy, Josephine with Peter McCarthy. *The Exorcist's Handbook.* Golem Media. 2010.

McCoy, Daniel. *The Viking Spirit: An Introduction To Norse Mythology and Religion.* CreateSpace Independent Publishing. 2016.

Miller, R. Michael. Josephine M. Harper. *The Psychic Energy Workbook: An Illustrated Course in Practical Psychic Skills.* Sterling Co. Inc. 1990.

Moss, Robert. *Dreamgates: Exploring the Worlds of Soul, Imagination, and Life Beyond Death.* New World Library. 1998, 2010.

Moss, Robert. *The Dreamer's Book of the Dead: A Soul Traveler's Guide To Death, Dying, and the Other Side.* Destiny Books. 2005.

Ogden, Daniel. *Greek and Roman Necromancy.* Princeton University Press. 2001.

Perry, Laura. *Shamanic Pathways- Deathwalking: Helping Them Cross the Bridge.* Moon Books. 2018.

Pinch, Geraldine. *Egyptian Mythology: A Guide To Gods, Goddesses, and the Traditions of Ancient Egypt.* Oxford University Press. 2002.

Rayor, Diane J. *The Homeric Hymns: A Translation, With Introduction and Notes.* University of California Press. 2004, 2014.

Regardie, Israel. *The Golden Dawn: The Original Account of the Teachings, Rites, and Ceremonies of the Hermetic Order of the Golden Dawn.* Llewellyn Publications.6th Edition. 2000.

Rollin, Tracey. *Santa Muerte: The History, Rituals, and Magic of Our Lady of the Holy Death*. Weiser Books. 2017.

Stoller, Galen. *My Life After Life: A Posthumous Memoir*. Dream Treader Press. 2011.

St. Pierre, Joellyn, D. Div. *The Art of Death Midwifery: An Introduction and Beginner's Guide*. BookSurge Publishing. 2009.

Tann, Mambo Chita. *Haitian Vodou: An Introduction to Haiti's Indigenous Spiritual Tradition*. Llewellyn Publications. 2012.

Thurman, Robert A.F. *The Tibetan Book of the Dead: Liberation Through Understanding In The Between*. Bantam Books. 1994.

Tymn, Michael. *The Afterlife Revealed: What Happens After We Die*. White Crow Books. 2011.

Tyson, Donald. *Scrying For Beginners*. Llewellyn Publications.1997.

Villoldo, Alberto. *Shaman, Healer, Sage: How To Heal Yourself and Others with Energy Medicine of the Americas*. Harmony Books. 2000.

Virgil. Translated by A. J. Kline. *Aeneid*. Poetry In Translation. 2015.

Warner, Felicity. *The Soul Midwives Handbook: The Holistic and Spiritual Care of the Dying*. Hay House Inc. 2013.

Websites

Choi, Charles Q. "Near-Death Experiences Shared By Science". *LiveScience.com* September 12, 2011. https://www.livescience.com/16019-death-experiences-explained.html.

Dhillon, Georgina. Editor. "Baron Samedi: A Loa of the Dead". *Kreolmagazine.com.* November 1, 2014. https://kreolmagazine.com/culture/history-and-culture/baron-samedi-a-loa-of-the-dead/#.XtVlacBOnIX

Dimitropoulos, Stav. "How Does Neuroscience Explain Spiritual and Religious Experiences?" *Medium.com*. August 19, 2017.

https://medium.com/s/spirits-in-your-brain/how-does-neuroscience-explain-spiritual-and-religious-experiences-3ef8c2f50339

Edmonds, Molly. "Is the brain hardwired for religion?" *HowStuffWorks.com*. September 22, 2018. https://science.howstuffworks.com/life/inside-the-mind/human-brain/brain-religion.htm

Edwards, Eric. "The Lore and Legend of the Black Dog". *Wordpress.com*. Eric Edwards Collected Works. https://ericwedwards.wordpress.com/2014/05/24/the-lore-and-legend-of-the-black-dog/

Frazier, Karen. "What Causes Poltergeist Activity?" *LoveToKnow.com*. http://www.assap.ac.uk/newsite/articles/Corner%20eye%20phenomena.html

Gessaman, Rhiannon. "The Soul Star Chakra: The Chakra You've Been Ignoring". October 17, 2017. https://astrologyanswers.com/article/the-soul-star-chakra-the-chakra-youve-been-ignoring/

Hopler, Whitney. "Archangel Michael Escorts Souls to Heaven." Learn Religions, Feb. 11, 2020, learnreligions.com/archangel-michael-escorting-souls-to-heaven-123842

LaMonica, Martin. "Are Near-Death Experiences Hallucinations? Experts Explain the Science Behind This Puzzling Phenomenon." *The Conversation*. December 4, 2018. https://theconversation.com/are-near-death-experiences-hallucinations-experts-explain-the-science-behind-this-puzzling-phenomenon-106286

Mark, Joshua J. "Anubis". *Ancient.eu*. July 25, 2016. https://www.ancient.eu/Anubis/

Mark, Joshua J. "Ghosts in the Ancient World". *Ancient.eu*. October 30, 2014. https://www.ancient.eu/ghost/

Townsend, Maurice. "Corner of the eye phenomena: shadow ghosts". *Assap.ac.uk*. 2009. http://www.assap.ac.uk/newsite/articles/Corner%20eye%20phenomena.html

**MOON
BOOKS**

PAGANISM & SHAMANISM

What is Paganism? A religion, a spirituality, an alternative belief system, nature worship? You can find support for all these definitions (and many more) in dictionaries, encyclopaedias, and text books of religion, but subscribe to any one and the truth will evade you. Above all Paganism is a creative pursuit, an encounter with reality, an exploration of meaning and an expression of the soul. Druids, Heathens, Wiccans and others, all contribute their insights and literary riches to the Pagan tradition. Moon Books invites you to begin or to deepen your own encounter, right here, right now. If you have enjoyed this book, why not tell other readers by posting a review on your preferred book site.

Recent bestsellers from Moon Books are:

Journey to the Dark Goddess
How to Return to Your Soul
Jane Meredith
Discover the powerful secrets of the Dark Goddess and
transform your depression, grief and pain into healing
and integration.
Paperback: 978-1-84694-677-6 ebook: 978-1-78099-223-5

Shamanic Reiki
Expanded Ways of Working with Universal Life Force Energy
Llyn Roberts, Robert Levy
Shamanism and Reiki are each powerful ways of healing; together,
their power multiplies. *Shamanic Reiki* introduces techniques to
help healers and Reiki practitioners tap ancient healing wisdom.
Paperback: 978-1-84694-037-8 ebook: 978-1-84694-650-9

Pagan Portals – The Awen Alone
Walking the Path of the Solitary Druid
Joanna van der Hoeven
An introductory guide for the solitary Druid, *The Awen Alone* will
accompany you as you explore, and seek out your own place
within the natural world.
Paperback: 978-1-78279-547-6 ebook: 978-1-78279-546-9

A Kitchen Witch's World of Magical Herbs & Plants
Rachel Patterson
A journey into the magical world of herbs and plants, filled with
magical uses, folklore, history and practical magic. By popular
writer, blogger and kitchen witch, Tansy Firedragon.
Paperback: 978-1-78279-621-3 ebook: 978-1-78279-620-6

Medicine for the Soul
The Complete Book of Shamanic Healing
Ross Heaven
All you will ever need to know about shamanic healing and how to
become your own shaman…
Paperback: 978-1-78099-419-2 ebook: 978-1-78099-420-8

Shaman Pathways – The Druid Shaman
Exploring the Celtic Otherworld
Danu Forest
A practical guide to Celtic shamanism with exercises and
techniques as well as traditional lore for exploring the Celtic
Otherworld.
Paperback: 978-1-78099-615-8 ebook: 978-1-78099-616-5

Traditional Witchcraft for the Woods and Forests
A Witch's Guide to the Woodland with Guided Meditations and
Pathworking
Mélusine Draco
A Witch's guide to walking alone in the woods, with guided
meditations and pathworking.
Paperback: 978-1-84694-803-9 ebook: 978-1-84694-804-6

Naming the Goddess
Trevor Greenfield
Naming the Goddess is written by over eighty adherents and
scholars of Goddess and Goddess Spirituality.
Paperback: 978-1-78279-476-9 ebook: 978-1-78279-475-2

Shapeshifting into Higher Consciousness
Heal and Transform Yourself and Our World with Ancient
Shamanic and Modern Methods
Llyn Roberts
Ancient and modern methods that you can use every day to
transform yourself and make a positive difference in the world.
Paperback: 978-1-84694-843-5 ebook: 978-1-84694-844-2

Readers of ebooks can buy or view any of these bestsellers by
clicking on the live link in the title. Most titles are published in
paperback and as an ebook. Paperbacks are available in traditional
bookshops. Both print and ebook formats are available online.

Find more titles and sign up to our readers' newsletter at
http://www.johnhuntpublishing.com/paganism
Follow us on Facebook at https://www.facebook.com/MoonBooks
and Twitter at https://twitter.com/MoonBooksJHP